# Truth
or Dare

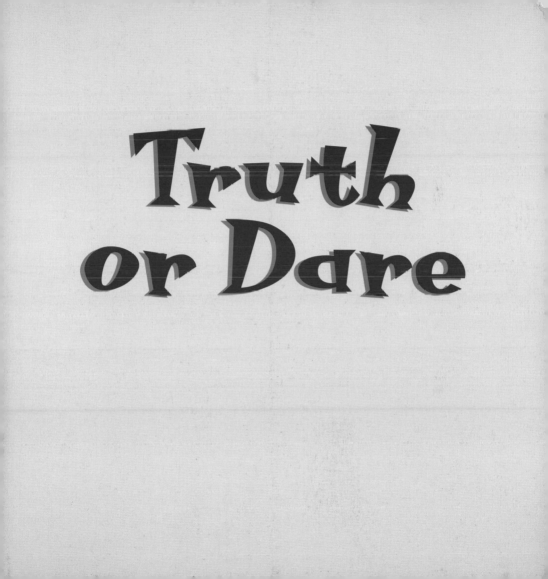

Warning: Small parts may be a choking hazard. Not for children under three years.

Disclaimer: The publisher and authors disclaim any liability from any injury that may result from the use, proper or improper, of the information contained in this book. Nothing in this book should be construed or interpreted to infringe on the rights of other persons or to violate criminal statutes: we urge you to obey all laws and respect all rights of others.

### ACKNOWLEDGEMENTS
A big thanks to all those daring enough to work on this project . . .
Writing/research team: Bob Moog, Erin Conley, Jenny Brennan, Cherie A. Martorana, and Maria Llull
Editing team: Bob Moog, Erin Conley, and Jenny Brennan.
Proofing team/barnyard censors: Heather Russell, Jenny Brennan,
Suzanne Cracraft, Rosie Slattery, Amanda Banks, and Erin Conley
Design/production team: Michael Friedman, Jeff Batzli, Rick Campbell, and Richela Morgan.
Sales and promotions team: Michael Friedman, Bruce Lubin, Mary Carlomagno, and Jules Herbert.
A special thanks to Ingrid Bell, Alison Bing, Jen Cho, Evelyn "Grandmommy" Conley, Michelle Conley,
Randy Conley, Regina Conley, Rick Conley, Lori Culwell, Beth Gilbert, Lisa Hamilton, Doug Hunt,
Sara Huong, Susan King, and Jennifer Spotts for their truthful tips, daring suggestions,
and knowing criticisms.
And finally, thanks to Francesca Araneta and Al Calmerin for their creative input.
We couldn't have done it without you—honestly!

Design: Lindgren/Fuller Design

ISBN 1-57528-906-7

03 04 MC 9 8 7 6 5 4 3

# CONTENTS

# INTRODUCTION

Who knows what I'd be doing now if I hadn't spent so much of my childhood playing games? Board games, card games, party games . . . I relished them all. I don't know of any activity that contributed to my development more than the nights I spent playing Truth or Dare (with the possible exception of strip poker). Truth or Dare taught me when to take a risk and when to play it safe. It also taught me a lot about my friends and myself. Games like Truth or Dare made me realize that you can learn lots and still have a good time. This realization inspired me to make fun and games my day job—and a way of life.

So take a chance and take a spin. No matter how old, or busy, or stressed you are, Truth or Dare is bound to bring out the kid in you!

Bob Moog

# Truth or Dare

**OBJECT** The aim of the game is to tell the truth, take some chances, and have fun with your friends while collecting points.

**PLAYING THE GAME** First things first: grab a pen and paper to keep track of your points.

- The oldest and wisest player spins first. After spinning, the player must read the first challenge spun (i.e. Truth, Dare, or Do You Know...) from Game 1, # 1 aloud to the group—and decide whether s/he wants to play or skip.
- *If a player decides to play a* **Truth or Dare** *challenge,* the group decides whether s/he earns a point—or NOT!

**TRUTH** = 1 point

**DARE** = 1 point

**DO YOU KNOW** = 1 bonus pass (These can be used to skip a challenge penalty free.)

- If a player decides to skip a **Truth or Dare** *challenge,* s/he loses a point—unless a bonus pass is traded in. There's no penalty if a player has 0 points and chooses to skip a challenge. Bonus passes held until the end of the game do not count toward final score.
- Play proceeds counterclockwise. Player 2 must now spin to see if s/he is up to the next challenge (and begins with Game 1, # 2).

**WINNING THE GAME** The first player to collect 10 points wins the game—honestly.

For added fun, see if you're slick enough to be part of the **Truth or Dare** Liar's Club!

# Truth or Dare

**TRUTH** You are a famous musician with a list of things that each concert venue must provide in your dressing room. What five things are on your list?

**DARE** Do a Michael Jackson "moonwalk" across the room.

**DO YOU KNOW...** which player can tell you what kind of currency you need to buy sushi in Japan?

—·—·—·—·—·—·—

**TRUTH** If you could have one physical characteristic from each player, what would it be?

**DARE** It's your very first recital. Give the tap-dancing performance of your life.

**DO YOU KNOW...** which player has never had a speeding ticket?

# Truth or Dare

**TRUTH** You've just won one million dollars! How much do you give to charity?

**DARE** Imitate the animal you hope to be in your next life.

**DO YOU KNOW...** which player would eat something s/he dropped on the floor?

— · — · — · — · — · —

**TRUTH** What would you do if you saw someone cheating on a test you were also taking?

**DARE** Congratulations! You just advanced to black belt. Demonstrate a sequence of karate movements for the other players.

**DO YOU KNOW...** how the player to your left likes his/her eggs?

# Truth or Dare

**TRUTH** A friend borrowed 10 bucks from you last week and still hasn't paid you back. Do you mention it to him/her?

**DARE** Let the player to your left put lipstick on you with his/her eyes closed.

**DO YOU KNOW...** which player leaves the smallest tips?

———————

**TRUTH** Your boss tells a dumb joke. Do you laugh?

**DARE** Cup your hands over your ears and record your verse for "We Are the World."

**DO YOU KNOW...** which player goes the longest without changing his/her socks?

# Truth or Dare

**TRUTH** If you could be any superhero, which one would you be?

**DARE** Pretend you're a lost puppy and convince another player to take you home.

**DO YOU KNOW...** which player spends the most time primping?

—·—·—·—·—·—

**TRUTH** Tell which player would be the best teacher.

**DARE** Pretend you're in bed having a nightmare.

**DO YOU KNOW...** which player is addicted to Internet chat rooms?

# Truth or Dare

**9**

**TRUTH** You're out to dinner and notice you weren't charged for your appetizer—do you tell your waiter?

**DARE** Name a famous person who looks like each player in your group.

**DO YOU KNOW...** what brand of toothpaste the player to your right usually uses?

—·—·—·—·—·—·—

**10**

**TRUTH** You are in a candy store, surrounded by jars of loose jellybeans—do you sample before you buy?

**DARE** Make the player to your left laugh any way you can in 30 seconds.

**DO YOU KNOW...** which player is the biggest procrastinator?

# Truth or Dare

**TRUTH** Describe what you looked like in 5th grade.

**DARE** You can't continue this relationship. Turn to the player on your right and break up with him/her.

**DO YOU KNOW...** which player makes lists to organize his/her day?

—·—·—·—·—

**TRUTH** Which player would most likely let your biggest secret slip?

**DARE** Name four U.S. states that begin with the word "New."

**DO YOU KNOW...** what day the person to your right was born?

# Truth or Dare

**13**

**TRUTH**  Which would be harder to give up: TV or chocolate?

**DARE**  Using only your nose, move a piece of fruit across the room.

**DO YOU KNOW...** what year the person to your right was born?

———·—·—·—·—

**14**

**TRUTH**  Which player tells the worst jokes?

**DARE**  Pick up three nearby objects and try to juggle them.

**DO YOU KNOW...** which player prefers a bath to a shower?

# Truth or Dare

**TRUTH** Do you think you have a good singing voice?

**DARE** Yodel 'til the other players tell you to stop.

**DO YOU KNOW...** which player owns the most shoes?

———————————

**TRUTH** If you could change your name, what would you change it to?

**DARE** Try to touch your nose with your tongue.

**DO YOU KNOW...** how many players have your home phone number memorized?

# Truth or Dare

**TRUTH** A young woman in a suit tells you she's lost her wallet and needs cab fare to the airport. What do you do?

**DARE** Draw a face on your stomach and make it say something to the player on your left.

**DO YOU KNOW...** which player likes anchovies?

— · — · — · — · — · —

**TRUTH** A cat darts into the road. You feel a thud under your tire. Do you stop?

**DARE** Give us your best snort!

**DO YOU KNOW...** what book the player to your left read most recently?

# Truth or Dare

**TRUTH** A friend has chronic bad breath. Do you say something? If so, what?

**DARE** You're the table. Have a conversation with the chair.

**DO YOU KNOW...** what type of cuisine the player to your left eats most often?

--- --- --- --- --- ---

**TRUTH** What kind of fruit best describes the player to your right, and why?

**DARE** Using your lips, pick up a pen off the floor.

**DO YOU KNOW...** when the player on your right last rode a bike?

# Truth or Dare

**TRUTH** What would you do if your best friend's significant other made a pass at you?

**DARE** Have an argument with yourself about what to have for dinner.

**DO YOU KNOW...** who eats the broccoli stems?

— · — · — · — · — · —

**TRUTH** If you had to move to another country for a year, which one would you choose, and why?

**DARE** You just won your first Academy Award®. Give your acceptance speech.

**DO YOU KNOW...** which players could add babysitting to their resume if they wished?

# Truth
## or Dare

**23**

**TRUTH**  If you could have invented something in history, including very recent history, what would it be and why?

**DARE**  You're a fashion critic at the Academy Awards® and the other players are movie stars. Give commentary on their outfits.

**DO YOU KNOW...** which player can roll his/her tongue?

— · — · — · — · —

**24**

**TRUTH**  If you only had 15 minutes left to live, what would you do?

**DARE**  You're auditioning for the lead in a movie about the player to your right. Try to be as convincing as you can. You want this part!

**DO YOU KNOW...** all of the other players' ages?

# Truth or Dare

**TRUTH** If you could remain one age for the rest of your life, what would it be?

**DARE** You're a superhero based on whatever object the player to your left hands you (i.e., "Pencil Man"/"Nacho Woman"). Get in character and tell us about your powers.

**DO YOU KNOW...** which player colors his/her hair?

—·—·—·—·—·—

**TRUTH** If your significant other and your pet were drowning, which one would you save?

**DARE** Tease your hair and sing your favorite song from the 1980s.

**DO YOU KNOW...** which player has sung karaoke most recently?

# Truth or Dare

**TRUTH** What's your biggest fear?

**DARE** Your head isn't screwed on right. Hold it in place for the next two minutes.

**DO YOU KNOW...** which player is the biggest junk food junkie?

— · — · — · — · —

**TRUTH** What kind of food is your best friend?

**DARE** Trade shoes and socks with the person to your left.

**DO YOU KNOW...** which player has a tattoo?

# Truth or Dare

**TRUTH** Ever tear up a bad photo of yourself? Describe the picture.

**DARE** Take off your shoes and socks and kiss both of your feet.

**DO YOU KNOW...** which player has a secret crush on a celebrity?

---

**TRUTH** What's the meanest thing you've done to a friend?

**DARE** Drop a piece of food on the floor, then pick it up and eat it.

**DO YOU KNOW...** which player has cheated on a test?

# Truth or Dare

**TRUTH** Name the best bad movie you ever loved.

**DARE** Give yourself a hickey on your arm.

**DO YOU KNOW...** which player has the smallest feet?

———·———·———·———·———

**TRUTH** What is your worst habit?

**DARE** Perform the cancan dance for the other players.

**DO YOU KNOW...** which player is an organ donor?

# Truth or Dare

**TRUTH** What's your favorite four-letter word?

**DARE** There's a new dance craze called the "Whiz Burger" sweeping the nation. Show us how it goes.

**DO YOU KNOW...** which player kisses his/her pet?

—·—·—·—·—·—

**TRUTH** If you could only take one player on a trip around the world, who would it be, and why?

**DARE** Call a friend and act like you think it's his/her birthday. Be sure to sing!

**DO YOU KNOW...** which player has run for office?

# Truth or Dare

**TRUTH** Have you ever borrowed somebody else's underwear?

**DARE** You're an unsuccessful Mafia boss and the player to your left is a priest. Confess.

**DO YOU KNOW...** which player is wearing dirty socks?

— — — — — — — — —

**TRUTH** Do you make friends easily?

**DARE** You're Kermit the Frog. Tell us why it's not easy being green.

**DO YOU KNOW...** how many players are wearing colored underwear?

# Truth or Dare

**TRUTH** Have you ever peed in a swimming pool?

**DARE** Pretend to lay a golden egg.

**DO YOU KNOW...** which players are left-handed?

—·—·—·—·—·—·—

**TRUTH** When you tell people how much you weigh, how close is it to the truth—in pounds?

**DARE** Let the player to your left draw glasses on you.

**DO YOU KNOW...** which players have had the chicken pox?

# Truth or Dare

**TRUTH** Which player is most likely to be a star?

**DARE** You just earned a lead in the school production of *Fame*. Give your best song and dance performance.

**DO YOU KNOW...** how many players have a parent born between 1934 and 1954?

———————

**TRUTH** Name the movie star you think you most resemble.

**DARE** Run across the room holding a book between your legs.

**DO YOU KNOW...** the favorite candy bar of the player on your left?

# Truth or Dare

**TRUTH** Describe your dream vacation. Where would you go? For how long? With whom?

**DARE** You are auditioning to be a stunt double. Show the group your most realistic stumble.

**DO YOU KNOW...** which player likes fruit-flavored water?

—·—·—·—·—·—

**TRUTH** Who is the most important person in the world to you?

**DARE** You are a flight attendant. Demonstrate some of the safety features of your aircraft.

**DO YOU KNOW...** where the player to your right's mother was born?

# Truth or Dare

**TRUTH** When is the last time you cried?

**DARE** Stick your head under the faucet.

**DO YOU KNOW...** which player likes fish sticks?

— · — · — · — · — · —

**TRUTH** What will the last line of your obituary say?

**DARE** Impersonate your favorite *Saturday Night Live* character.

**DO YOU KNOW...** which player orders buttered popcorn at the movies?

# Truth or Dare

**TRUTH** What was your first job? How much were you paid?

**DARE** Pull up your nose and oink like a hungry pig.

**DO YOU KNOW...** what each player prefers: a hot dog, a hamburger, or tofu?

—·—·—·—·—·—

**TRUTH** What literary character do you most relate to, and why?

**DARE** Call a friend and ask if you can borrow 60 cents.

**DO YOU KNOW...** which player can name all four members of the *Scooby-Doo*® gang? (Answer: Fred, Daphne, Velma, and Shaggy)

# Truth or Dare

**TRUTH** What would be the best thing about being the opposite sex?

**DARE** You're the newest Spice Girl. Tell us your name and perform one of the group's songs.

**DO YOU KNOW...** the name(s) of the player to your right's sibling(s)?

— - — - — - — - —

**TRUTH** Tell which Brady you'd date if you had to.

**DARE** Put your finger in your ear, then lick your finger.

**DO YOU KNOW...** how to spell each player's last name?

# Truth or Dare

**TRUTH** Ever get caught cheating? Give details.

**DARE** Phone a friend and ask for advice about whether or not you should invest in a new pair of socks.

**DO YOU KNOW...** which player is double-jointed?

—··—··—··—··—··—

**TRUTH** Describe the most spontaneous thing you've ever done. Did you regret it? Why or why not?

**DARE** Pick a nearby object and "show-and-tell" it to the group.

**DO YOU KNOW...** which player leaves the toilet seat up?

# Truth or Dare

**TRUTH** How often do you shower?

**DARE** It's karaoke time! Sing a couple lines of Nelly Furtado's "I'm Like a Bird."

**DO YOU KNOW...** which player can speak a foreign language?

— · — · — · — · — · —

**TRUTH** Which player would you say was the cutest baby?

**DARE** You're a robot. Dance and sing at least one chorus of "Mr. Roboto."

**DO YOU KNOW...** which player talks in his/her sleep?

# Truth or Dare

**TRUTH** How much money do you have in the bank?

**DARE** Rub noses with the player of your choice.

**DO YOU KNOW...** which player is a shopaholic?

---

**TRUTH** If you had to give birth in a cab, which player would you want to play doctor?

**DARE** Keep your eyes closed for an entire round.

**DO YOU KNOW...** which player can count to ten in Spanish?

# Truth or Dare

**TRUTH** Which player would you hate to have as a boss?

**DARE** Recite the theme song to a cartoon chosen by the player across from you as though it were Shakespearean verse.

**DO YOU KNOW...** which player bites his/her nails?

———————

**TRUTH** What's your favorite part of your body?

**DARE** Pick the player in the group you think would "go easiest" on you and do whatever s/he dares you to do.

**DO YOU KNOW...** the favorite drink of the player to your right?

# Truth
# or Dare

**TRUTH** While waiting on a very rude customer, you accidentally drop his bread onto the floor in the kitchen. Do you serve it to him?

**DARE** Compliment the player to your left using only words that begin with the letter "M."

**DO YOU KNOW...** which player has had stitches?

--·-·-·-·-·-·-·-

**TRUTH** Name the movie you would star in if you could be the lead in any film ever made.

**DARE** Pretend to milk a cow.

**DO YOU KNOW...** which player has had a perm?

# Truth or Dare

**TRUTH** Who would you call for advice if you had questions about love?

**DARE** Pretend the player to your left is Elmo and tickle him/her.

**DO YOU KNOW...** which players believe in ghosts?

—·—·—·—·—·—

**TRUTH** If you had to give up one of the five senses (sight, hearing, touch, smell, or taste), which one would it be?

**DARE** Pretend you're in the shower and pantomime what you'd be doing. Keep it clean!

**DO YOU KNOW...** which players have ever been in a play or musical?

# Truth or Dare

**TRUTH**   Your new boy/girlfriend baked you a birthday cake that tastes like glue. What do you do?

**DARE**   Call a friend and tell him/her how excited you are about this week's ketchup sale at the grocery store.

**DO YOU KNOW…** which player has hay fever?

—·—·—·—·—·—·—·—

**TRUTH**   What is the most valuable lesson you've ever learned?

**DARE**   There's a new dance craze called the "Funky Turtle" sweeping the nation. Show us how it goes.

**DO YOU KNOW…** which players have been to Europe?

# Truth
# or Dare

**TRUTH**  What sport would you like to play professionally?

**DARE**  Speak the chorus to a well-known love song into the player on your left's ear.

**DO YOU KNOW...** which player has had the most afterschool detentions?

--------

**TRUTH**  Ever opened someone else's email and read it without telling them?

**DARE**  You're a New York socialite. Greet the other players and give each a big fake kiss on the cheek.

**DO YOU KNOW...** which player likes peas?

# Truth or Dare

**TRUTH** Which movie star would you most like to have a romantic scene with?

**DARE** Sing "Raindrops Keep Falling on My Head" and let the player to your left flick water at you.

**DO YOU KNOW...** which player has been bungee jumping?

- - - - - - - -

**TRUTH** What player's phone would you most like to tap?

**DARE** Do your best Grinch imitation and steal something from one of the other players.

**DO YOU KNOW...** which player is the youngest?

# Truth or Dare

**TRUTH** What's the worst thing a friend has ever done to you?

**DARE** You're a butterfly about to hatch from your cocoon. Show us the metamorphosis.

**DO YOU KNOW...** which player has seen a Broadway show?

— · — · — · — · — · —

**TRUTH** If you could give your parents any one gift in the world, what would it be?

**DARE** Say "and I've got gas" after everything you say for the next three minutes.

**DO YOU KNOW...** which player has eaten a bug?

# Truth or Dare

**TRUTH** Which player is most likely to sneak a peek at his/her birthday gift?

**DARE** Let the player to your left draw a tattoo that says "I [heart] Mom" on your forearm.

**DO YOU KNOW...** which player can breakdance—and will prove it?

—·—·—·—·—·—

**TRUTH** If the player to your left were a city, which one would s/he be? Why?

**DARE** Eat a cracker and whistle your favorite tune.

**DO YOU KNOW...** which player tends to burn toast?

# Truth or Dare

**TRUTH** Tell the player to your left something that bugs you about him/her.

**DARE** Pluck a strand of hair from your head and floss your teeth with it. (If your hair is too short, use another player's.)

**DO YOU KNOW...** which player likes the smell of gasoline?

—·—·—·—·—·—

**TRUTH** What do you feel most guilty about?

**DARE** Beatbox a rhythm you can dance to.

**DO YOU KNOW...** which player interrupts people the most?

# Truth or Dare

**73**

**TRUTH** Name the one person (famous or not) that you'd like to trade places with for one day.

**DARE** Lie down on your stomach and pull yourself across the room using only your elbows.

**DO YOU KNOW...** which player cleans his/her plate—and everyone else's?

—·—·—·—·—·—

**74**

**TRUTH** Which player is most likely to talk his/her way out of a speeding ticket?

**DARE** It's your final performance of *Riverdance*. Show us how it's done!

**DO YOU KNOW...** which player has wet his/her pants in the last ten years?

# Truth or Dare

**TRUTH** What's the last good deed someone's done for you?

**DARE** You're a Golden Retriever. Using your mouth, fetch something nearby and drop it in the player to your right's lap.

**DO YOU KNOW...** which player knows where SpongeBob Squarepants lives? (Answer: Bikini Bottom)

—·—·—·—·—·—■

**TRUTH** What is your least favorite fashion trend?

**DARE** You're Tweety Bird™. Tell the other players why you'd make a great twuck driver.

**DO YOU KNOW...** which player reads the tabloids?

# Truth or Dare

**TRUTH** What is the closest you've been to having your 15 minutes of fame?

**DARE** Pretend that you're blowing up a really, really large balloon.

**DO YOU KNOW...** which player isn't home splitting atoms on the weekends?

—·—·—·—·—·—

**TRUTH** Do you think you have a guardian angel? If so, when is the last time you think it was watching over you?

**DARE** Touch your ears with your feet any way you can.

**DO YOU KNOW...** which player collects things and what does s/he collect?

# Truth or Dare

**TRUTH** If you needed a transplant and could clone anyone's heart, whose heart would it be?

**DARE** Perform a short gymnastics floor routine while singing the chorus to Van Halen's "Jump."

**DO YOU KNOW...** which player actually read the *Lord of the Rings* before seeing the movie?

— · — · — · — · — · —

**TRUTH** What is your favorite city?

**DARE** Give your best interpretation of a chick hatching from its egg.

**DO YOU KNOW...** which player has a fear of heights?

# Truth or Dare

**TRUTH** If you could have anyone's wardrobe, whose would you choose?

**DARE** You've just met the person you want to spend the rest of your life with. Practice your heartfelt proposal on the player to your left.

**DO YOU KNOW...** which player has never changed a baby's diaper?

—·—·—·—·—·—·—

**TRUTH** If you could change the mind of one person on one issue, whose mind and what issue would it be?

**DARE** You're Bart Simpson. Bend over and sing "A Spoonful of Sugar Helps the Medicine Go Down."

**DO YOU KNOW...** which player has the whitest teeth?

# Truth or Dare

**TRUTH** If you could wipe out one word or phrase, what would it be?

**DARE** You're Kenny G. Play the sax using your thumb as the mouthpiece.

**DO YOU KNOW...** which player takes a bite of his/her cookie before reading the fortune?

—————————

**TRUTH** If you had triplet daughters today, what would you name them?

**DARE** It's St. Patrick's Day and you forgot to wear green. Let each player show you the consequences.

**DO YOU KNOW...** which player has a food allergy?

# Truth or Dare

**85**

**TRUTH** If you found a bag of money in a parking lot, what would you do?

**DARE** The player to your right is a cop. You're the suspect. Let him/her frisk you.

**DO YOU KNOW...** the number of candles that appeared on the player to your left's last birthday cake?

— · — · — · — · —

**86**

**TRUTH** Name one thing that always makes you smile.

**DARE** Sing the "Beans, Beans the Magical Fruit" song. Wrap it up with a big fake toot!

**DO YOU KNOW...** what the player to your left had for breakfast this morning?

# Truth or Dare

**TRUTH** What is the one thing you wish you had the guts to tell your mother or father?

**DARE** Call someone on the phone and try to sell him/her a nose-hair clipper.

**DO YOU KNOW...** which player looks like his/her mom?

—————————

**TRUTH** Which player would make the best talk show host?

**DARE** Describe what you did yesterday—in Shakespearean English.

**DO YOU KNOW...** which player prefers bacon bits to croutons on his/her salad?

# Truth or Dare

**TRUTH** Describe a time when you put your foot in your mouth.

**DARE** Say the names of everyone in the room along with the very first word that comes into your head.

**DO YOU KNOW...** which player has at least one silver filling?

—·—·—·—·—·—

**TRUTH** If you could communicate with any type of animal, which would you pick?

**DARE** Pretend you're a cow and chew your cud.

**DO YOU KNOW...** which players have been caught falling asleep in class by a teacher?

# Truth or Dare

**91**

**TRUTH** What is the one subject in school that you think is the most useful?

**DARE** Make your belly button sing "The Star Spangled Banner."

**DO YOU KNOW...** which players have played "Light as a Feather, Stiff as a Board"?

———————————

**92**

**TRUTH** Which player is most likely from outer space?

**DARE** Reenact a scene from your favorite movie, playing all the parts yourself.

**DO YOU KNOW...** which player has called a psychic hotline?

# Truth or Dare

**TRUTH**  Tell which player's mood ring would change color most often.

**DARE**  Sing the show tune of your choice at top volume while tap dancing.

**DO YOU KNOW...** which player gives him/herself a pep talk before stressful situations (i.e., dates or public speaking engagements)?

---

**TRUTH**  Describe your worst-ever fashion moment.

**DARE**  Make up a new last name for everyone in the room.

**DO YOU KNOW...** which player is a *Survivor* diehard?

# Truth or Dare

**TRUTH** Describe a time when you caught someone in a lie.

**DARE** Invent a new dance move, then teach it to everyone in the room. Be sure to give it a name!

**DO YOU KNOW...** which player color-codes his/her closet?

— · — · — · — · — · —

**TRUTH** What's the one food you absolutely can't stand, and why?

**DARE** Reenact your favorite music video and have the other players guess which one it is.

**DO YOU KNOW...** which player can do the best Elvis impersonation?

# Truth or Dare

**TRUTH** Which player is most likely to use a cheesy pick-up line?

**DARE** There's a new dance craze called the "Sloppy Joe" sweeping the nation. Show us how it goes.

**DO YOU KNOW...** which player rarely packs a lunch?

---

**TRUTH** Describe a time you passed gas out loud—and you weren't alone.

**DARE** Make up a children's nursery rhyme involving a duck, a cookie, a pair of scissors, and the player to your right.

**DO YOU KNOW...** which players prefer Coke® to Pepsi®?

# Truth or Dare

**TRUTH** When is the last time you slept with a stuffed animal?

**DARE** Get up and dance and sing like James Brown.

**DO YOU KNOW...** which player had a bowl haircut when s/he was younger?

———————————

**TRUTH** How can people tell when you're lying?

**DARE** Pretend that you're a clown entertaining a group of five-year-olds at a birthday party.

**DO YOU KNOW...** which player has had his/her current hairstyle the longest?

# Truth or Dare

**TRUTH** What do you do about pimples—pop them or just wait until they dry up?

**DARE** You are a tree that has just fallen victim to the woodcutter's axe. Timber!

**DO YOU KNOW...** which player is a tree hugger?

—·—·—·—·—·—·—

**TRUTH** Which player would be the best inspiration for a Diva® doll?

**DARE** You're a fly. Buzz around the room and annoy the other players.

**DO YOU KNOW...** which player can name at least one Judy Blume book?

# Truth or Dare

**TRUTH** Do you look inside the tissue after you blow your nose?

**DARE** Bark and beg like a dog.

**DO YOU KNOW...** which player needs to go to confession?

—·—·—·—·—·—

**TRUTH** Have you ever picked food out of the garbage—and eaten it?

**DARE** Lie on your back and pedal your feet in the air for 30 seconds. (Your bottom should not be touching the ground.)

**DO YOU KNOW...** which player has been to the Grand Canyon?

# Truth or Dare

**TRUTH** Do you think you'll make a good parent? Why? If you already are a parent, are you the parent you thought you'd be?

**DARE** Pretend that you're in bed having a really, really great dream.

**DO YOU KNOW...** which player likes to horseback ride?

—·—·—·—·—·—

**TRUTH** A person in front of you tosses a Styrofoam cup on the ground. What do you do?

**DARE** There's a new dance craze called the "Ham Hair" sweeping the nation. Show us how it goes.

**DO YOU KNOW...** the color of the other players' eyes? No looking!

# Truth or Dare

**TRUTH** Have you ever scraped the mold off moldy food and eaten it?

**DARE** Pretend you're being struck by lightning at this very moment!

**DO YOU KNOW...** which player would pick up a hitchhiker?

— · — · — · — · — · — · —

**TRUTH** Have you ever sniffed your underwear to see if it was clean?

**DARE** Using your whole body (not just your arms), shape yourself into the letter "U."

**DO YOU KNOW...** which player can do a convincing sick voice?

# Truth or Dare

**TRUTH**  Tell the story behind one of your scars.

**DARE**  Stuff a pillow up your shirt and pretend to go into labor.

**DO YOU KNOW...** which player would rather wait for the movie than read the book?

— · — · — · — · — · —

**TRUTH**  You've been waiting in line at the bank for what seems like hours. An elderly woman in a wheelchair cuts in front of you. What do you do?

**DARE**  You've just been cast in a "Joy of Prune Juice" commercial. Act it out for us.

**DO YOU KNOW...** which player can bench-press a small child?

# Truth or Dare

**TRUTH** Your new friend wears enough dime-store cologne to choke a horse. Do you tell him?

**DARE** There's a new dance craze called the "Shuggie Otis" sweeping the nation. Show us how it goes.

**DO YOU KNOW...** which player took tap-dancing lessons as a kid?

— · — · — · — · — · —

**TRUTH** Your bank statement says you have an extra $500 in your account. Do you tell the bank?

**DARE** Using a mirror, take a pen and write the player to your right's name on your forehead.

**DO YOU KNOW...** which player has read *The Catcher in the Rye*?

# Truth or Dare

**TRUTH** Have you ever spied on someone? Who? Why?

**DARE** With all of your heart, audition for the next big teeny-bopper band.

**DO YOU KNOW...** which player could stop a runaway camel?

—·—·—·—·—·—

**TRUTH** Which player's hair would you most like to have?

**DARE** As fast as you can, talk nonstop about whatever comes into your head for one full minute. No stopping!

**DO YOU KNOW...** which player always asks, "Do I have food in my teeth?"

# Truth or Dare

**TRUTH** Would you date someone just for his/her money?

**DARE** You're a famous singer and the player to your left is one of your biggest fans. Serenade him/her with your sappiest hit.

**DO YOU KNOW...** which player aspires to see his/her name in lights?

_._._._._._._

**TRUTH** Name a has-been actor or musician that you had (or still have!) a huge crush on.

**DARE** Teach the other players how to country line dance, even if you don't know how to.

**DO YOU KNOW...** which player thinks beef jerky is a tasty treat?

# Truth or Dare

**TRUTH** You've just had a lousy date. Do you say it was nice or tell the truth?

**DARE** Using at least five words, make up a tongue twister starting with an S.

**DO YOU KNOW...** which player hates the holidays?

---

**TRUTH** What advice would you give to your child if s/he was being pushed around by the school bully?

**DARE** Do a rain dance.

**DO YOU KNOW...** which player was breast-fed as a baby?

# Truth or Dare

**119**

**TRUTH** If you could have center stage at Madison Square Garden for one hour, what would you do?

**DARE** Sing your school song or do a team cheer.

**DO YOU KNOW...** which player feels the need to forward chain-letter e-mails?

— · — · — · — · — · —

**120**

**TRUTH** If you had proof that your friend was having an affair with the married governor of your state, would you tell the press or keep it to yourself?

**DARE** Show everyone your driver's license/photo I.D.

**DO YOU KNOW...** which player knows who wrote *Oh, The Places You'll Go!*?

# Truth or Dare

**TRUTH** If a joke is told and everyone but you seems to "get it," do you pretend that you get it too, or ask the person who told it to explain?

**DARE** Let the player to your right make up a dare for you.

**DO YOU KNOW...** which players have had their teeth cleaned in the last six months?

—·—·—·—·—·—

**TRUTH** Have you ever picked (your nose) and flicked?

**DARE** Do your best imitation of the motormouth donkey from *Shrek*.

**DO YOU KNOW...** what the player to your left's favorite TV show is?

# Truth or Dare

**TRUTH** If you had to pick one player to spend a year on a deserted island with, who would you pick?

**DARE** Pretend you are a pirate and start every sentence with "Ay, matey" until your next turn.

**DO YOU KNOW...** the first name of the player to your left's dad?

—·—·—·—·—·—

**TRUTH** Which of the Ten Commandments have you broken most recently?

**DARE** Walk like a penguin.

**DO YOU KNOW...** which player has a minivan in his/her future?

# Truth or Dare

**125**

**TRUTH** How old were you when you stopped believing in Santa Claus?

**DARE** Do your best impersonation of a blowfish and swim around the room three times.

**DO YOU KNOW...** which player has the biggest backyard?

— · — · — · — · — · — · —

**126**

**TRUTH** You've been offered a dream job that will double your salary, but you'll have to move to a remote island for three years. Do you accept?

**DARE** Pretend your hands are puppets and put on a show for the other players.

**DO YOU KNOW...** which player uses AOL®?

# Truth
## or Dare

**TRUTH** You're working on project for a big client. An hour before deadline, you spill soda on your disk and lose everything. What do you tell your client?

**DARE** Communicate only in writing until your next turn.

**DO YOU KNOW...** which player needs to trim his/her toenails?

— · — · — · — · — · —

**TRUTH** Have you ever passed gas—and blamed it on someone else?

**DARE** You're golfing and your ball is two feet away from the 18th hole. Sink it!

**DO YOU KNOW...** which player would win an all-night dance marathon?

# Truth or Dare

**TRUTH** Describe the best vacation you've ever had.

**DARE** Without speaking, tell the story of your life while doing the hula.

**DO YOU KNOW...** which player won't use the bathroom in a public place?

--- --- --- --- ---

**TRUTH** Name one thing your parents are proud of you for.

**DARE** Do the chicken dance. Don't know it? Do it anyway.

**DO YOU KNOW...** who takes the longest showers?

# Truth or Dare

**131**

**TRUTH** What would the legal driving age be if you were setting it?

**DARE** Imitate your favorite cartoon character.

**DO YOU KNOW...** which player has "forgotten" to return a pair of bowling shoes?

––––––––––––

**132**

**TRUTH** What was your favorite book when you were a kid?

**DARE** Do five one-handed pushups.

**DO YOU KNOW...** which player can name both of his/her state senators?

# Truth or Dare

**133**

**TRUTH** Name something one of your friends has that you wish were yours.

**DARE** Make the silliest face you can and accompany it with sound effects.

**DO YOU KNOW...** which player is a WWF fan?

—·—·—·—·—·—

**134**

**TRUTH** Name the main purpose you think you were put on this earth.

**DARE** Give the person next to you a shoulder rub using your elbows.

**DO YOU KNOW...** which player is guilty of using catchphrases?

# Truth or Dare

**TRUTH** If you could eliminate one form of weather, what would it be?

**DARE** Show off your midriff while singing a Britney Spears or Madonna tune.

**DO YOU KNOW...** which player has had the most exotic pet?

— · — · — · — · — · —

**TRUTH** If you could eliminate a single type of animal, which would you choose? Why?

**DARE** Finish the limerick about the player to your left "I once had a friend from Van Beezer." (Remember limericks have five lines!)

**DO YOU KNOW...** which players are wearing shoes that lace? No looking!

# Truth
# or Dare

**TRUTH** What's the worst gift you've ever given?

**DARE** Write a brief anonymous note telling the neighbors how much you enjoy living next door to them. Now put it in their mailbox.

**DO YOU KNOW...** which player can tell you which movie won this year's Academy Award® for Best Picture?

—·—·—·—·—·—

**TRUTH** If you could have any store added to your local mall, which one would it be?

**DARE** In a foreign accent, whisper something into the ear of another player.

**DO YOU KNOW...** which player can tell you who played Gertie in *E.T.*? (Answer: Drew Barrymore)

# Truth or Dare

**TRUTH** Name the most beautiful place you've ever seen.

**DARE** You're a big juicy steak. Let each player take a bite.

**DO YOU KNOW...** which player knows in what month we celebrate Earth Day? (Answer: April)

---

**TRUTH** Name the most unsung hero you know of.

**DARE** Without speaking, act out your three favorite Olympic sports.

**DO YOU KNOW...** which player laughs when s/he is nervous?

# Truth or Dare

**TRUTH**  Have you ever been really thankful for your life? Describe that moment.

**DARE**  In one breath, sing for as long as you can at the highest pitch you can reach.

**DO YOU KNOW...** which player has been to Graceland?

— · — · — · — · — · —

**TRUTH**  Describe the most memorable night of your life.

**DARE**  Pour soda (or another sticky liquid) into your bellybutton.

**DO YOU KNOW...** which player likes meatloaf?

# Truth
# or Dare

**TRUTH** Name the grossest thing you have ever put in your mouth (on purpose or not).

**DARE** Spit water in the air and try to catch it in your mouth.

**DO YOU KNOW...** which player has been in the longest relationship?

—·—·—·—·—·—·—

**TRUTH** Describe your favorite childhood memory.

**DARE** Pretend to make out with yourself in the corner.

**DO YOU KNOW...** which player can name four characters on *Star Trek*?

# Truth or Dare

**145**

**TRUTH** If you had a rare bone marrow that matched that of a dying acquaintance in need of a transplant, would you donate it?

**DARE** You just got a new job at the baseball park selling hot dogs and peanuts. Let's see you in action.

**DO YOU KNOW...** which player can tell you what candy uses the slogan "Taste the rainbow"? (Answer: Skittles®)

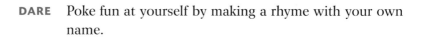

**146**

**TRUTH** If life unfolded exactly as you'd like, where would you be in one year?

**DARE** Poke fun at yourself by making a rhyme with your own name.

**DO YOU KNOW...** which player doesn't separate darks and lights when washing clothes?

# Truth or Dare

**TRUTH** You're on the phone with a heartbroken friend when your biggest crush calls on the other line—do you click over to answer?

**DARE** Pretend to be the player to your right until your next turn.

**DO YOU KNOW...** which player played in a softball/baseball league when s/he was younger?

—·—·—·—·—·—

**TRUTH** If you could tell your boss/teacher one thing without any consequences, what would it be?

**DARE** Lick your elbow.

**DO YOU KNOW...** which player can tell you on what game show contestants are asked to "Come on down!"? (Answer: *The Price Is Right*)

GAME 2

# Truth or Dare

**TRUTH** Describe the most extravagant purchase you've ever made, and tell exactly how much you paid for it.

**DARE** Imitate Porky Pig s-s-singing "I Got You Babe."

**DO YOU KNOW...** which player has the most change in his/her pockets or purse?

—— ·· —— ·· —— ·· —— ·· —— ·· ——

**TRUTH** Grandma gives you an ugly sweater. What do you do— wear it, toss it, or give it to the next friend that has a birthday?

**DARE** Serenade the player you know least well with a Broadway show tune.

**DO YOU KNOW...** which player still sleeps with a stuffed animal?

# Truth or Dare

**TRUTH** Which player would you peg as a schoolyard bully?

**DARE** There's a new dance craze called the "Tiger Woods Swing" sweeping the nation. Show us how it goes.

**DO YOU KNOW...** which player will take clothing out of the dirty clothes hamper to wear?

— - — - — - — - — - —

**TRUTH** If you could hypnotize someone for one day, who would it be and what would you have him/her do?

**DARE** Hold hands with another player until your next turn.

**DO YOU KNOW...** which player can name at least one local newscaster?

# Truth
# or Dare

**TRUTH** You are introduced to the president of the United States. What one thing do you want to say to him?

**DARE** Let the player on your right draw a tattoo on your shoulder.

**DO YOU KNOW...** who didn't shower today?

— · — · — · — · — · — · —

**TRUTH** You've got spring fever and it's a perfect day to spend outside. Do you play hooky?

**DARE** Let the player of your choice draw a flower around your bellybutton.

**DO YOU KNOW...** which player got mostly "As" in school?

# Truth or Dare

**TRUTH** The lottery jackpot has reached $80 million. Do you buy a ticket?

**DARE** Take off another player's sock with your teeth.

**DO YOU KNOW...** which player goes to church regularly?

— · — · — · — · — ·

**TRUTH** Which player is most likely to peek out from under the blindfold when playing Blind Man's Bluff?

**DARE** In one word, describe the personality of the player to your right.

**DO YOU KNOW...** which player watches soap operas?

# Truth or Dare

**TRUTH** Which player is most likely to share his/her lunch?

**DARE** Use a different pickup line on each player.

**DO YOU KNOW...** which player knows the difference between a Rob Roy and a Shirley Temple?

—·—·—·—·—·—

**TRUTH** You are on the Titanic as it's sinking. There's one life vest left for you and your closest friend. What do you do?

**DARE** Tell the player to your right something that bugs you about him/her.

**DO YOU KNOW...** what kind of lunchbox the player to your right carried in grade school?

# Truth or Dare

**TRUTH** You get great service from your local coffee shop. You notice a tip jar is on the counter—do you leave a tip?

**DARE** Read the player to your right's palm and predict his/her future.

**DO YOU KNOW...** the player to your left's middle name?

—·—·—·—·—·—

**TRUTH** Which player's pet do you like the least?

**DARE** Demonstrate the first five ballet positions. If you don't know them, make them up.

**DO YOU KNOW...** what month the person to your left was born?

# Truth or Dare

**TRUTH** You're home alone and run out of toilet paper. What do you do?

**DARE** Do 20 push-ups. Have the other players count down.

**DO YOU KNOW...** the last TV show seen by the person on your left?

—·—·—·—·—·—

**TRUTH** Which player would be least likely to survive if stranded on a desert island?

**DARE** There's a new dance craze called the "G-Dubya" sweeping the nation. Show us how it goes.

**DO YOU KNOW...** which player has the biggest feet?

# Truth or Dare

**15**

**TRUTH** A car in the parking lot has its lights on — what do you do?

**DARE** Draw a fake moustache on yourself and wear it home tonight.

**DO YOU KNOW...** the home phone number of the player to your right by heart?

—·—·—·—·—·—

**16**

**TRUTH** If the player to your left were a tree, which kind would s/he be: an Oregon crab apple, an American oak, or a sugar maple?

**DARE** Drink three eight-ounce glasses of water before your next turn.

**DO YOU KNOW...** something that is under the player on your left's bed?

# Truth or Dare

 **17**

**TRUTH**  If you could talk to one person, dead or alive, who would it be?

**DARE**  Scream "I love pink leather" out the window.

**DO YOU KNOW...** who flosses daily?

———·——·—·——·——

 **18**

**TRUTH**  If you could move to one place for the rest of your life, where would it be?

**DARE**  Stick your tongue out and wink at the same time.

**DO YOU KNOW...** what the player to your left's favorite board game is?

# Truth
# or Dare

**TRUTH** Tell the group the name of your imaginary childhood friend.

**DARE** Make out with the nearest pillow.

**DO YOU KNOW...** what the player to your right's dream car is?

— · — · — · — · — · —

**TRUTH** You're a star. What's your stage name?

**DARE** Pretend you're Malibu Barbie and tell us why you're dumping Ken.

**DO YOU KNOW...** what color house or apartment building the player to your right lives in?

# Truth or Dare

**TRUTH** Which player would be the best business partner and why?

**DARE** Call a friend and pretend that s/he is the one who called you.

**DO YOU KNOW...** which players are the youngest children in their families?

—·—·—·—·—·—

**TRUTH** If you were stranded on a deserted island with only one CD to listen to, which one would it be?

**DARE** There's a new dance craze called the "Midnight Snack" sweeping the nation. Show us how it goes.

**DO YOU KNOW...** what was the first concert the player to your left attended?

# Truth or Dare

**TRUTH** Which player is most likely to walk into a sliding glass door?

**DARE** You are running for president of the United States. Give a speech and see how many votes you can win.

**DO YOU KNOW...** which player prefers bran flakes to frosted flakes for breakfast?

—·—·—·—·—·—·—

**TRUTH** If your house were in flames and you could only grab one thing, what would it be?

**DARE** Give everyone in the group a nickname that rhymes with his/her real name.

**DO YOU KNOW...** what wish the player to your right would make if today were his/her birthday?

# Truth
# or Dare

**TRUTH**  Confess a white lie that you've told to someone in the group.

**DARE**  The player to your right is a cop and has just pulled you over for speeding. Talk your way out of the ticket.

**DO YOU KNOW...** which player reads the newspaper every day?

**TRUTH**  Name the player you could take down most easily in a no-holds-barred fight.

**DARE**  You're running for 6th grade president. Give us your speech.

**DO YOU KNOW...** which players had braces?

# Truth or Dare

**TRUTH** Name a song you're embarrassed to admit you like.

**DARE** Belch as much of the alphabet as you can.

**DO YOU KNOW...** which player snores?

— · — · — · — · — · — · —

**TRUTH** Who have you flirted with most recently?

**DARE** Pretend that you've just put a large spoonful of peanut butter in your mouth and tell us about your day.

**DO YOU KNOW...** which player has an "outie" bellybutton?

# Truth
# or Dare

**TRUTH** Which player is the biggest flirt?

**DARE** Channel the spirit of Elvis Presley and let him speak through you, baby.

**DO YOU KNOW...** the favorite cartoon character of the player to your right?

—·—·—·—·—·—·—

**TRUTH** Which player do you think would plan the most creative date?

**DARE** Sniff the player to your left's shoe.

**DO YOU KNOW...** how many keys the player to your left has on his/her key chain?

# Truth or Dare

**TRUTH** Which player most needs his/her mouth washed out with soap?

**DARE** Pretend you're a cat and give yourself a "bath."

**DO YOU KNOW...** which player has read a *Harry Potter* book?

---

**TRUTH** What word is most embarrassing for you to say?

**DARE** Sit on the ground and try to put one leg behind your head.

**DO YOU KNOW...** which player has donated blood?

# Truth or Dare

**TRUTH** Who was your first love?

**DARE** Let the player to your left make up a dare for you.

**DO YOU KNOW...** which player played soccer as a kid?

– · – · – · – · – · –

**TRUTH** Tell about a time when you laughed inappropriately.

**DARE** Pick another player to stand behind you and let yourself fall back into his/her arms.

**DO YOU KNOW...** which player still holds a candle for a long-lost flame?

# Truth or Dare

**35**

**TRUTH**  What's the most fun you've had after midnight?

**DARE**  You're a mime in a box. Show us how you get out.

**DO YOU KNOW...** which player talks to him/herself when home alone?

———·—·—·—·—·—

**36**

**TRUTH**  When is the last time you felt left out?

**DARE**  Balance a spoon on your nose for at least three seconds.

**DO YOU KNOW...** which player can name all of the Seven Dwarfs?

# Truth or Dare

**TRUTH** How much money would it take to get you to run around the block naked?

**DARE** Don't use your thumbs for the next five minutes.

**DO YOU KNOW...** the name(s) of the pet(s) belonging to the person on your right?

---

**TRUTH** Have you ever had a crush on a friend's boy/girlfriend?

**DARE** Imitate the evil Hobbit, Gollum, from *Lord of the Rings*.

**DO YOU KNOW...** which player has the most pennies in his/her pocket?

# Truth
## or Dare

**TRUTH** What's your favorite word or phrase?

**DARE** Pretend you're Winnie the Pooh, stick out your belly, and sing "I'm so rumbly in my tumbly. Time to munch an early luncheon, time for something sweet!"

**DO YOU KNOW...** the favorite flower of the player to your right?

— - — · — · — · — · — · —

**TRUTH** What makes you happy?

**DARE** With your head back, arms out, and eyes closed, walk as if you're on a tight rope.

**DO YOU KNOW...** the favorite painter of the player on the left?

# Truth or Dare

**TRUTH** What's your best quality?

**DARE** Do your most annoying laugh until someone in the group tells you to stop.

**DO YOU KNOW...** which player has a birthmark?

_._._._._._._

**TRUTH** What's the first thing you thought of when you woke up this morning?

**DARE** Do 20 jumping jacks while singing "Eye of the Tiger" from _Rocky._

**DO YOU KNOW...** what is the ethnic background of the player to your left?

# Truth or Dare

**TRUTH** What one word do you want to be described with after you die?

**DARE** There's a new dance craze called the "Spunky Brewster" sweeping the nation. Show us how it goes.

**DO YOU KNOW...** what is the astrological sign of the player to your left?

———————————

**TRUTH** What movie do you quote most often? Prove it.

**DARE** Belt out a verse of "Stairway to Heaven" as if you were an opera singer.

**DO YOU KNOW...** which player can tell you who played Princess Leia in *Star Wars?*

# Truth or Dare

**TRUTH** Who do you most admire? Why?

**DARE** Ask your neighbor if you can borrow a pair of socks.

**DO YOU KNOW...** which player writes in block print?

—·—·—·—·—·—

**TRUTH** Which *Seinfeld* character do you identify with most, and why?

**DARE** Make art out of something in the trash and try to sell it to the player to your left.

**DO YOU KNOW...** which player likes black licorice?

# Truth
## or Dare

**TRUTH** If you had to get back together with an ex, which one would it be? Why?

**DARE** It's karaoke time! Sing a couple lines of Pink's "Get the Party Started."

**DO YOU KNOW...** which players can crack their knuckles?

— · — · — · — · — · —

**TRUTH** Name three things you look for in a mate.

**DARE** Phone a friend and wish him/her "Happy Belly Button Appreciation Day."

**DO YOU KNOW...** how many pets the player to your left has?

# Truth or Dare

**TRUTH** Describe the worst hairstyle you've ever had.

**DARE** Pull one hair out of your head for each person playing, excluding yourself.

**DO YOU KNOW...** what color underwear the player to your right is wearing?

—·—·—·—·—

**TRUTH** What is your biggest addiction?

**DARE** Pretend you're Hello Kitty® and convince the player to your left that you hate Pokémon.

**DO YOU KNOW...** which player can play a musical instrument?

# Truth or Dare

**TRUTH** Ever think you might have ESP (extrasensory perception)?

**DARE** Lead the group in a meditation on the beauty of "invisible" scotch tape.

**DO YOU KNOW...** which player prefers veggies over meat?

—·—·—·—·—·—

**TRUTH** Who did you vote for in the last presidential election? If you didn't vote, who would you have chosen if you did?

**DARE** Keep whatever edible item the player to your left chooses in your back pocket until the end of the game.

**DO YOU KNOW...** which player snorts when they laugh?

# Truth
# or Dare

**TRUTH** Have you ever pretended to be someone else in a chat room?

**DARE** Put an ice cube on your head and keep it there until it melts.

**DO YOU KNOW...** which player can water-ski?

_._._._._._

**TRUTH** Has anyone ever walked in on you in the bathroom?

**DARE** Open up, say "Ahh!", and let everyone get a good look at your dental work.

**DO YOU KNOW...** which player is least likely to forgive you after a fight?

# Truth or Dare

**TRUTH** Describe the time your mother or father embarrassed you most.

**DARE** Stand up and recite the Pledge of Allegiance. Come on, you should know this! Make it up if you have to.

**DO YOU KNOW...** the player to your left's favorite food?

———————————————

**TRUTH** Do you think you're a lucky or an unlucky person?

**DARE** There's a new dance craze called the "Englebert Humperdink" sweeping the nation. Show us how it goes.

**DO YOU KNOW...** which player drinks straight from the milk carton?

# Truth or Dare

**TRUTH** What is the one thing you'd change about your childhood, if you could?

**DARE** Using only gestures, signal to your Wall Street trader to buy more pork bellies.

**DO YOU KNOW...** which players have broken a bone?

—·—·—·—·—·—

**TRUTH** Name the one book you would like to have with you if you were stranded on a desert island.

**DARE** You've been told to walk the plank. Now beg and plead your way out of it, you scurvy pirate.

**DO YOU KNOW...** which player has mowed lawns for money?

# Truth or Dare

**TRUTH**  If you could be any animal in your next life, what animal would you come back as?

**DARE**  Try to convince the player to your left to buy your shirt for more than it's worth. Sell it!

**DO YOU KNOW...** which player believes that there is life on other planets?

———————

**TRUTH**  Name the one superpower you'd like to have.

**DARE**  You're the CEO of a failing dot-com and the other players are investment bankers. Convince them to pour more money into your sinking ship.

**DO YOU KNOW...** which player is a *Buffy the Vampire Slayer* buff?

# Truth or Dare

**TRUTH** If you could eliminate one form of prejudice from the world, what would it be?

**DARE** Sing a well-known disco song as if it were a solemn hymn.

**DO YOU KNOW...** which player has the most stamps on his/her passport?

---

**TRUTH** Who would you call if you were kidnapped and allowed only one phone call?

**DARE** Phone a friend and ask if you can borrow an ice cube.

**DO YOU KNOW...** which player has gotten a new pair of shoes in the last three months?

# Truth or Dare

**TRUTH** Ever read someone else's diary? Share the details.

**DARE** Pretend you're the Queen of England and knight the player to your left.

**DO YOU KNOW...** which player was a cheerleader?

—·—·—·—·—·—

**TRUTH** How much time do you spend on your hair every day?

**DARE** Do your best boy band dance.

**DO YOU KNOW...** what year the player to your left started kindergarten?

# Truth or Dare

**TRUTH** If you could be invisible for one day, where would you go, and what would you do?

**DARE** Let the player to your left mess up your hair.

**DO YOU KNOW...** which player is the biggest pack rat?

---

**TRUTH** What trait would you like to pass on to your kids?

**DARE** You're a baby dinosaur about to hatch. Show us the miracle of life.

**DO YOU KNOW...** which player is the oldest?

# Truth or Dare

**TRUTH** If you could trade houses with someone in the room, who would it be?

**DARE** You're a snake about to molt. Slither across the room and shed your skin.

**DO YOU KNOW...** which player has tried escargot?

—·—·—·—·—·—

**TRUTH** Would you lick the seat of a public toilet for a thousand bucks?

**DARE** Say "She sells seashells by the sea shore" five times.

**DO YOU KNOW...** which player knows what a turkey baster is for?

# Truth
# or Dare

**TRUTH** Describe a dream you had about another player, but never shared.

**DARE** Say "and I just let one fly" after everything you say for the next five minutes.

**DO YOU KNOW...** who's a Mac lover and who's a PC lover?

—·—·—·—·—·—

**TRUTH** If the player to your right were a car, which one would s/he be? Why?

**DARE** You've just come across the player to your right's diary. Read a juicy passage out loud to the group.

**DO YOU KNOW...** which players have been to the opera?

# Truth or Dare

**TRUTH** Have you ever hung up on somebody? Share the details.

**DARE** Do the worm across the room.

**DO YOU KNOW...** which player prefers plain M&M's® to peanut?

—·—·—·—·—·—

**TRUTH** If you could go back in time and witness one event from your family's history, what would it be?

**DARE** You're on fire! Stop, drop, and roll across the room.

**DO YOU KNOW...** which player likes to play video games?

# Truth or Dare

**TRUTH** Name the one household chore that you wish you never had to do again.

**DARE** Cross the length of the room as fast as you can without using your feet.

**DO YOU KNOW...** which players say "God bless you" after someone sneezes?

---

**TRUTH** What breed would you be if you were reincarnated as a dog?

**DARE** Give another player a piggyback ride across the room.

**DO YOU KNOW...** which players have been on TV?

# Truth or Dare

 **75**

**TRUTH** If you could name only one song as the best song of all time, which would it be?

**DARE** You're a horse. Take the player to your left for a ride around the room.

**DO YOU KNOW...** which player has cut his/her own hair?

— · — · — · — · — · —

 **76**

**TRUTH** Describe a time you were fooled on April Fool's Day.

**DARE** David Letterman is watching. Do your best stupid human trick.

**DO YOU KNOW...** which player watches infomercials?

# Truth or Dare

**TRUTH** Describe a perfect evening.

**DARE** Give the group a "tour" of the contents of your pockets.

**DO YOU KNOW...** which player can tell you what the teenage sleuths in *Scooby-Doo* call their van? (Answer: The Mystery Machine)

———————

**TRUTH** If you could have a magic red button on your desk that did one thing when you pressed it, what would you want that thing to be?

**DARE** Go cross-eyed.

**DO YOU KNOW...** which player can juggle?

# Truth or Dare

**TRUTH** Who would you change places with if you could pick one person in the world?

**DARE** Close your eyes, cross your arms, bend your knees, and balance on one foot for 30 seconds without falling.

**DO YOU KNOW...** which player is the biggest kid at heart?

———————————

**TRUTH** Name one person you would like to know better.

**DARE** Take the player to your left's next dare—no matter what it is.

**DO YOU KNOW...** which player can list the most U.S. capitals in one minute? (Have players write down answers as you time them to see if your guess is correct!)

# Truth
# or Dare

**TRUTH** What's the worst song you could wake up to?

**DARE** Recite "Peter Piper picked a peck of pickled peppers" as quickly as you can 10 times.

**DO YOU KNOW...** which player has gone fishing?

———————

**TRUTH** Who is the most charming person you've ever met?

**DARE** Nibble on your big toe.

**DO YOU KNOW...** which players go for Letterman and which go for Leno?

# Truth or Dare

**TRUTH** If you could prevent one person from overusing one word/phrase, who and what would it be?

**DARE** Pretend you're Captain Underpants and tell us about your superpowers.

**DO YOU KNOW...** which player has read the book *and* seen the movie *The Princess Diaries*?

**TRUTH** If you had triplet sons today, what would you name them?

**DARE** Do your best bull in a china shop imitation.

**DO YOU KNOW...** which player is most likely to end up with a lamp shade on his/her head at the end of the evening?

# Truth or Dare

**TRUTH** Who's the most gullible person in the room?

**DARE** You're in the library. Whisper till your next turn.

**DO YOU KNOW...** which player would rather snack than sit down to a meal?

---

**TRUTH** What's the biggest mistake you've ever made?

**DARE** Do an interpretive dance that expresses your feelings about the player to your right.

**DO YOU KNOW...** which players used to like Barney?

# Truth or Dare

**TRUTH** How old do you wish you were right now?

**DARE** Go ring your neighbor's doorbell. When someone answers, smile and say "Trick or Treat!"

**DO YOU KNOW...** which player looks like his/her dad?

---

**TRUTH** Describe a time you acted like a real dork

**DARE** Come up with a pet "love" name (i.e., schmoopy, pumpkin) for everyone in the room.

**DO YOU KNOW...** which player would make the best lifeguard?

# Truth or Dare

**TRUTH**  What is your most prized possession?

**DARE**  Pick all the lint out of your belly button, then show it to everyone in the room.

**DO YOU KNOW...** which players would eat pizza that's been sitting out overnight for breakfast?

—·—·—·—·—·—·—

**TRUTH**  What's the nicest compliment anyone's ever given you?

**DARE**  There's a new dance craze called the "Dumplet" sweeping the nation. Show us how it goes.

**DO YOU KNOW...** which player can tell you the name of J-Lo's first album? (Answer: *On the Six*)

# Truth or Dare

**TRUTH** What is the one subject in school that you think is the least useful?

**DARE** Do a dramatic re-enactment of the first time you met the person to your right.

**DO YOU KNOW...** which player owns a pair of roller blades?

—·—·—·—·—·—·—

**TRUTH** If you could have one TV sitcom house as your real home, which would you pick?

**DARE** Identify one thing the player to your left has that you want, then beg him/her for it.

**DO YOU KNOW...** which player needs the TV on to fall asleep?

# Truth or Dare

**93**

**TRUTH**  Tell your juiciest secret.

**DARE**  Give each player a World Wrestling Federation (WWF) name and persona.

**DO YOU KNOW...** which player can name at least three members from the most recent *Real World* cast?

———————

**94**

**TRUTH**  If the player to your left were a bird, what species would s/he be: a cuckoo, a kingfisher, or a chickadee?

**DARE**  Go into the bathroom and come out wearing your underwear over your pants.

**DO YOU KNOW...** which player irons his/her jeans?

# Truth
# or Dare

**95**

**TRUTH** If the person sitting to your left were an animal, what animal would s/he be and why?

**DARE** Give a sales pitch for adult diapers to the group.

**DO YOU KNOW...** which player can tell you what U.S. ice-skater scored gold at the Salt Lake City winter Olympics in 2002? (Answer: Sarah Hughes)

— · — · — · — · — · — · —

**96**

**TRUTH** Have you ever told someone you got a bad grade on a test when you really aced it?

**DARE** Sing the highest note you can sing.

**DO YOU KNOW...** which player blushes easily?

# Truth
# or Dare

**TRUTH** Who in the group has a sibling or relative you would like to date?

**DARE** Rub your stomach and pat your head at the same time.

**DO YOU KNOW...** which players own an item purchased from QVC?

--- --- --- --- ---

**TRUTH** Have you ever lied about how much you paid for something?

**DARE** Drink everyone's beverage, including your own. Then be polite and replenish their drinks.

**DO YOU KNOW...** what item of clothing would you never see the person to your left wearing?

# Truth or Dare

**TRUTH** Name three things you wouldn't do for money.

**DARE** Pretend you're a robot and short circuit.

**DO YOU KNOW...** which player has had his/her hair cut most recently?

— - — - — - — - — -

**TRUTH** Do you always remember to say please and thank you?

**DARE** You've just won the prestigious award for "Florist of the Year." Let's hear your acceptance speech, please.

**DO YOU KNOW...** which player saw *Titanic* sink more than once?

# Truth or Dare

**TRUTH** Have you ever "borrowed" someone else's clothes—and never returned them?

**DARE** There's a new dance craze called the "Praying Mantis" sweeping the nation. Show us how it goes.

**DO YOU KNOW...** which player is most conservative?

— · — · — · — · — · —

**TRUTH** How old were you when you gave up your security blanket?

**DARE** Quack and waddle like a duck.

**DO YOU KNOW...** which player wears his/her heart on his/her sleeve?

# Truth or Dare

**TRUTH** Did you ever want something belonging to a friend so badly that you thought about stealing it? What was it? What did you end up doing?

**DARE** Applaud everything that the player to your right says for the next two rounds.

**DO YOU KNOW...** which player would rather live with mice than kill them?

———————————

**TRUTH** When was the last time you cut in line?

**DARE** Play an imaginary harp.

**DO YOU KNOW...** which player is the most competitive?

# Truth or Dare

**105**

**TRUTH** Which player has claustrophobia?

**DARE** You're skydiving for the first time. Check your parachute and jump!

**DO YOU KNOW...** which players have ever been handcuffed?

---

**106**

**TRUTH** If a good friend asked you to take a test for him so he could graduate, and you knew you wouldn't get caught, would you do it?

**DARE** The player across from you is the president of the U.S. Salute and say, "Hail the Chief!" for the next five minutes every time s/he speaks.

**DO YOU KNOW...** which player knows his/her neighbors on a first-name basis?

# Truth or Dare

**TRUTH** Have you ever sniffed your socks to see if they were clean?

**DARE** Shape your body into the letter "P."

**DO YOU KNOW...** which player can name five of the Smurfs?

—·—·—·—·—·—

**TRUTH** What's the biggest lie you've ever told?

**DARE** Do the "Bump" with your chair.

**DO YOU KNOW...** which player thinks skiing is for dorks?

# Truth or Dare

**TRUTH** Name five dishes you could make using only the ingredients on the top shelf in the refrigerator.

**DARE** Pretend you're a Christmas tree and decorate yourself.

**DO YOU KNOW...** which player plucks his/her eyebrows?

—·—·—·—·—·—

**TRUTH** Walking in the park, you notice a dog owner not pick up after his dog. What do you do?

**DARE** Your dentures just fell out! Talk without them till your next turn.

**DO YOU KNOW...** which player has a green thumb?

# Truth or Dare

**TRUTH** What word or phrase would you like to eliminate from one of the other player's vocabulary?

**DARE** Make up a joke about a firefighter in a wax museum.

**DO YOU KNOW...** which player was a Girl/Boy Scout?

_._._._._._

**TRUTH** Your grandmother invites you over for a special birthday celebration on the same night your favorite band is playing in town. What do you do?

**DARE** Let the player to your left use your lap as a footrest for your next two turns.

**DO YOU KNOW...** which player thinks s/he has big ears?

# Truth or Dare

**TRUTH** What's the best award you've ever won?

**DARE** Pretend that you're insane and the other players have come to visit you in your padded cell.

**DO YOU KNOW...** which player could climb the corporate ladder the fastest?

———·—·—·—·—·—

**TRUTH** Would you eat an earthworm for a thousand bucks?

**DARE** You're from another planet and you've never seen a human being before. Describe the player across from you to the "folks" back home.

**DO YOU KNOW...** which player still listens to the Spice Girls?

# Truth or Dare

**TRUTH** A cute guy/girl who is spoken for is flirting with you. What do you do?

**DARE** Crow like a rooster at the break of day.

**DO YOU KNOW...** which player wouldn't be caught dead driving a minivan?

---

**TRUTH** If you receive someone else's mail by mistake, do you throw it away or give it back to the mail carrier?

**DARE** Teach the other players how to swim the breaststroke.

**DO YOU KNOW...** which player has a gag reflex?

# Truth
# or Dare

**TRUTH** You've just had a lousy date. What do you do when s/he leans in for a good night kiss?

**DARE** Pretend you're holding a crying baby that won't be soothed, no matter what you do.

**DO YOU KNOW...** which player can quote a line from *The Breakfast Club*?

—·—·—·—·—·—

**TRUTH** Have you ever deliberately tried to make a boy/girlfriend jealous?

**DARE** You just drank Love Potion No. 9! It will affect you till you spin again.

**DO YOU KNOW...** which player can quote a line from *Star Wars*?

# Truth or Dare

**TRUTH** If your best friend was wanted by the police, would you help him/her hide and/or flee the state?

**DARE** Pretend to be the player to your left until your next turn.

**DO YOU KNOW...** which player knows who voiced Princess Fiona in *Shrek*? (Answer: Cameron Diaz)

— · — · — · — · —

**TRUTH** If you could be any fictional literary character for a week, who would you be?

Dare Spin a quarter on the table and stop it with your finger without tipping it over. Do it until you get it right.

**DO YOU KNOW...** which player has got a bad habit of being late?

# Truth
## or Dare

**TRUTH** Your neighbors get the Sunday paper and you don't. If you know that they're gone until Monday, do you take their paper?

**DARE** Do "The Timewarp" from *The Rocky Horror Picture Show*. Don't know it? Do it anyway.

**DO YOU KNOW...** which players flossed last night?

—·—·—·—·—·—

**TRUTH** While the person sitting next to you on the plane is in the bathroom, you spill your drink on his/her seat. Do you say anything?

**DARE** Do your best Air Jordan.

**DO YOU KNOW...** which player has the most $1 bills in his/her wallet?

# Truth or Dare

**TRUTH** If you and the other players were starring in a TV show, which one would it be?

**DARE** Remain completely silent until your next turn.

**DO YOU KNOW...** the first name of the player to your right's mom?

—·—·—·—·—·—

**TRUTH** Your friend wrote a book. You think it's terrible, but it's getting rave reviews. Do you tell your friend what you think?

**DARE** Name the state capital of Washington, D.C.

**DO YOU KNOW...** which player always remembers to wear sunscreen?

# Truth or Dare

**125**

**TRUTH**  A friend tells an off-color joke. What do you do?

**DARE**  Act like an angry mime until your next turn.

**DO YOU KNOW...** which player has a cell phone?

———·—·—·—·—·—·—

**126**

**TRUTH**  You meet what you think could be your soul mate only to find it's your roommate's ex. Do you pursue?

**DARE**  Pretend you're a cow with the deepest voice in the pasture and moo "Old MacDonald."

**DO YOU KNOW...** who belts out songs when driving alone?

# Truth
# or Dare

**TRUTH**  You're late for an important meeting. The only open space in front of the office is reserved for handicapped parking. What do you do?

**DARE**  Laugh in an exaggerated, obnoxious manner at everything the player to your left says until your next turn.

**DO YOU KNOW...** which players drink diet soda and which drink regular?

— · — · — · — · — · —

**TRUTH**  If you could have season tickets for any team, any sport, in any spot in the stadium, which team would it be, and where would you sit?

**DARE**  Sing the chorus of a current pop song to the group.

**DO YOU KNOW...** which player ordered pizza most recently?

# Truth or Dare

**TRUTH** If you did not have to go to school or work, what would a typical day be like for you?

**DARE** Get down on all fours, wag your behind, and sing "How Much Is That Doggy in the Window?"

**DO YOU KNOW...** what number the player to your left considers his/her lucky number?

—·—·—·—·—·—

**TRUTH** When's the last time you made your parents really mad?

**DARE** Act like a monkey.

**DO YOU KNOW...** what the player to your right considers his/her biggest weakness?

# Truth or Dare

**TRUTH** Have you ever had the same dream twice? What was it about?

**DARE** Get down on all fours and imitate a scared cat.

**DO YOU KNOW...** which player has the most expensive sunglasses?

--------

**TRUTH** Name one person you wish you were still friends with.

**DARE** Stand on your head in a yoga position for one minute.

**DO YOU KNOW...** which player is a slave to fashion?

# Truth or Dare

**133**

**TRUTH** If you could pair up any two people you know, whom would you pick?

**DARE** Pour a glass of water over your head.

**DO YOU KNOW...** which player takes time to stop and smell the roses?

— · — · — · — · —

**134**

**TRUTH** If you found out for sure that there is no such thing as an afterlife, how would you change your life?

**DARE** You've just invented three-legged pantyhose. Convince the player to your left to buy a pair.

**DO YOU KNOW...** which section of the bookstore you'd most likely find the player to your right in?

# Truth or Dare

**TRUTH** Name the one person you are most jealous of.

**DARE** Hum a well-known rock anthem or heavy metal song until someone guesses it.

**DO YOU KNOW...** which player does his/her own laundry?

—·—·—·—·—·—·—

**TRUTH** What's your favorite type of American accent, other than your own?

**DARE** Do your best bellydance.

**DO YOU KNOW...** which players are not wearing socks? No peeking!

# Truth or Dare

**TRUTH** What's the best gift you've ever given?

**DARE** You're Chicken Little. Scurry nervously around the room repeating "The sky is falling" 10 times.

**DO YOU KNOW...** which player can tell you which movie won this year's Academy Award® for Best Foreign Film?

— · — · — · — · — · —

**TRUTH** Tell about a time you were mean to your sibling(s).

**DARE** You are auditioning for a spot in a cold and sinus reliever commercial. Fake a triple sneeze attack.

**DO YOU KNOW...** which player knows what it means to shoot a birdie in golf?

# Truth or Dare

**TRUTH** If you could have one type of snack always stocked up in your kitchen cupboard, what would it be?

**DARE** Blow your best spit bubble.

**DO YOU KNOW...** which players prefer chocolate to vanilla?

---

**TRUTH** What is your definition of love?

**DARE** Stuff a pillow down your pants and do the "Rump Shaker" dance.

**DO YOU KNOW...** which player has a TV in his/her bedroom?

# Truth
# or Dare

**141**

**TRUTH** If you had ten thousand dollars in counterfeit money and a 1% chance of getting caught, would you use the money?

**DARE** Draw a flower on your forehead without using a mirror.

**DO YOU KNOW...** which player has seen the movie *Ice Age*?

—·—·—·—·—·—

**142**

**TRUTH** Describe your most embarrassing moment.

**DARE** Give a sales-pitch for a new product called the "Hankyshmelt" to the group.

**DO YOU KNOW...** which player knows the first verse of the "Star Spangled Banner"?

# Truth or Dare

**TRUTH** Name the person who has been on your mind most in the past few days.

**DARE** The person on your left is your therapist. Have a two-minute session with him/her describing a problem in your life.

**DO YOU KNOW...** which player could clean house in a game of pool?

— · — · — · — · — · —

**TRUTH** What is the most spontaneous thing you have ever done?

**DARE** Use any two items as chopsticks to successfully pick up a penny from the floor.

**DO YOU KNOW...** which player knows how to play poker?

# Truth or Dare

**TRUTH** What is one question you are afraid to ask because you know you won't like the answer?

**DARE** Let the player to your left crack your knuckles for you.

**DO YOU KNOW...** which player has had athlete's foot?

—·—·—·—·—·—

**TRUTH** If life unfolded exactly as you'd like, where would you be in five years?

**DARE** Tell a story that involves a fish, a clock, a priest, and a hot dog.

**DO YOU KNOW...** which player is better at talking than listening?

# Truth
## or Dare

**TRUTH** You see an old man trip and fall. Do you stop to help?

**DARE** Convince the other players that you should be the next pope.

**DO YOU KNOW...** which player has been thrown a surprise party?

— · — · — · — · — · —

**TRUTH** If you had a voodoo doll, who would you cast a spell on?

**DARE** Pick another player and show and tell him/her to the group.

**DO YOU KNOW...** which player had Colorforms® when s/he was a kid?

GAME 3

# Truth or Dare

**TRUTH** If you found $1,000 in an unmarked wallet on the street, what would you do?

**DARE** Stand in front of the group and sing "Happy Birthday, Mr. President" à la Marilyn Monroe.

**DO YOU KNOW...** which player can tell you who won the last *Survivor* show?

---

**TRUTH** If someone wrote a book based on the life of the person to your left, what would the title be?

**DARE** Do your best imitation of *Seinfeld*'s Kramer.

**DO YOU KNOW...** who failed his/her first driver's test?

# Truth or Dare

**TRUTH** Which player would be the best roommate? Why?

**DARE** Arm wrestle with the player to your left.

**DO YOU KNOW...** which player has played hooky most recently?

— · — · — · — · — · —

**TRUTH** Fifteen minutes after leaving the house, you realize you forgot to turn off the iron. What do you do?

**DARE** Draw a portrait of the player to your left.

**DO YOU KNOW...** the street address of the player to your right?

# Truth or Dare

**5**

**TRUTH**  Your grandmother suffers double-kidney failure. You're the closest match. Do you donate a kidney?

**DARE**  There's a new dance craze called the "Top Ramen" sweeping the nation. Show us how it goes.

**DO YOU KNOW...** which player is most likely to skip down the block?

—·—·—·—·—·—·—

**6**

**TRUTH**  Your mom and best friend are drowning but you have time to save only one—which one do you rescue?

**DARE**  Pretend you're a pigeon in heat and woo another player.

**DO YOU KNOW...** which player knows what kind of dog *Scooby-Doo* is? (Answer: Great Dane)

# Truth or Dare

**TRUTH** The waiter apologizes after spilling soup in your lap, but doesn't offer to comp the meal. Do you leave a tip?

**DARE** The players to your left and right are getting married. Stand up and give them their wedding toast.

**DO YOU KNOW...** which player can tell you what funnyman married the actress who played Marcia Brady in the movies? (Answer: Ben Stiller)

—·—·—·—·—·—

**TRUTH** Describe a time when you recognized a person on the street, but pretended not to know him/her.

**DARE** Give the player to your left a nickname and use it for the next five minutes.

**DO YOU KNOW...** which player has special ordering down to a science?

# Truth or Dare

**TRUTH** Which player is least likely to share his/her lunch?

**DARE** There's a new dance craze called the "Rumplet" sweeping the nation. Show us how it goes.

**DO YOU KNOW...** the color of the player to your left's toothbrush?

—·—·—·—·—·—

**TRUTH** How do you think you will know who you're going to marry?

**DARE** Bark a Christmas carol.

**DO YOU KNOW...** which players have a cordless phone?

# Truth or Dare

**TRUTH** You just remembered you forgot your significant other's birthday (after the fact). How do you make up for it?

**DARE** Greet each member in the group without using the word hello—and use each greeting no more than once.

**DO YOU KNOW...** which player makes his/her bed every day?

---

**TRUTH** You step in dog-doo. What is the first thing that comes out of your mouth?

**DARE** You've made it to the national body-building championship. Show us your trophy-winning performance.

**DO YOU KNOW...** which player sings in the shower?

# Truth or Dare

**TRUTH** You dent the car parked next to you in the lot as you swing open your door. What do you do?

**DARE** Do 20 sit-ups. Have the other players count down.

**DO YOU KNOW...** which player usually eats dinner in front of the TV?

— - — - — - — - —

**TRUTH** Describe your ideal mate.

**DARE** Do the splits.

**DO YOU KNOW...** which player has smelly feet?

# Truth
# or Dare

**TRUTH** Your future in-laws make your least favorite dish for dinner. What do you do?

**DARE** Burp the vowels.

**DO YOU KNOW...** which player prefers dill pickles over sweet pickles?

—————————————

**TRUTH** Which player is most likely to return the gift you got him/her?

**DARE** Speak only in rhyme until your next turn.

**DO YOU KNOW...** who's known who the longest in the group?

# Truth
# or Dare

**TRUTH** What's the craziest thing you've done to get someone to notice you?

**DARE** Speak in Pig Latin and tell the player to your left that there's a fly in his/her soup.

**DO YOU KNOW...** which player often skips breakfast?

— · — · — · — · — · —

**TRUTH** A friend gets a really bad haircut. What is your response?

**DARE** Tell us your best joke.

**DO YOU KNOW...** which player bites his/her fingernails?

# Truth or Dare

**TRUTH** Describe the worst argument you've ever had with a friend.

**DARE** Say "and I love to wear tight underwear" after everything you say for the next five minutes.

**DO YOU KNOW...** which player's never been dumped?

- - - - - - - -

**TRUTH** What would you do for a living, if you could do anything you wanted?

**DARE** Think of five words that rhyme with thirst. (It's harder than it seems.)

**DO YOU KNOW...** what astrological sign the player to your right is?

# Truth or Dare

**TRUTH** Which player is most likely to live the longest?

**DARE** Build a sculpture using the other players as your clay. Be sure to give your work a title.

**DO YOU KNOW...** what time is usually bedtime for the player to your right?

---

**TRUTH** If forced to choose, would you eat wet or dry cat food?

**DARE** Sing the lowest note you can sing.

**DO YOU KNOW...** which player is not afraid of snakes?

# Truth or Dare

**23**

**TRUTH** Which would be harder to do without: the phone or the computer?

**DARE** Show everyone in the room how good you are at breakdancing.

**DO YOU KNOW...** which player has taken piano lessons?

—·—·—·—·—·—

**24**

**TRUTH** If someone made a movie about your life, what would they call it? Who would you want to play you?

**DARE** There's a new dance craze called the "Parking Job" sweeping the nation. Show us how it goes.

**DO YOU KNOW...** which player reads his/her horoscope?

# Truth or Dare

**TRUTH** If you could take back one thing in your life, what would it be?

**DARE** Confess your most ticklish spot and let the player to your left tickle you there.

**DO YOU KNOW...** which player screens his/her calls?

— · — · — · — · — · —

**TRUTH** Tell which player is most likely to offer his/her seat on the bus to an elderly person.

**DARE** Speak in a heavy Scottish brogue until your next turn.

**DO YOU KNOW...** which player has the most fillings?

# Truth or Dare

**TRUTH** What teen idol would you most like to date?

**DARE** There's a new dance craze called the "Fish Finger" sweeping the nation. Show us how it goes.

**DO YOU KNOW...** which player has been in a car accident?

———————

**TRUTH** Tell which player you'd vote most likely to succeed.

**DARE** Count to 60 by threes in less than two minutes.

**DO YOU KNOW...** which player sleeps with his/her socks on?

# Truth or Dare

**TRUTH** Ever get caught stealing? Give details.

**DARE** Do three cartwheels in a row.

**DO YOU KNOW...** which player watches *SpongeBob Squarepants*?

— · —· — · —· — · —

**TRUTH** Ever get caught lying? Give details.

**DARE** Pretend you are a chicken and cluck "Happy Birthday."

**DO YOU KNOW...** which player hates to talk on the phone?

# Truth
# or Dare

**TRUTH** Ever broken the law? Describe how.

**DARE** Impersonate one of the other players until someone in the group guesses who you're supposed to be.

**DO YOU KNOW...** which player is the shortest?

---

**TRUTH** How well do your parents really know you? How well do you know them?

**DARE** Recite the alphabet backwards.

**DO YOU KNOW...** which players would rather be cremated than buried?

# Truth or Dare

**TRUTH** If the player to your left were a reptile, what kind would s/he be: a jungle gecko, a box turtle, or a frilled dragon?

**DARE** There's a new dance craze called the "Pooper-Scooper" sweeping the nation. Show us how it goes.

**DO YOU KNOW...** which player has been on a blind date?

———·——·——·——·——

**TRUTH** What's the worst thing you've ever cooked?

**DARE** Pretend you're a goat on a job interview. Sell yourself.

**DO YOU KNOW...** which player is most embarrassed by this game?

# Truth or Dare

**TRUTH** Have you ever picked something out of your teeth and eaten it?

**DARE** Shape your body into the letter "R."

**DO YOU KNOW...** which player was/is the teacher's pet?

—·—·—·—·—·—

**TRUTH** When was the last time you changed your sheets?

**DARE** Pretend that the rest of the group is a band and you're their groupie.

**DO YOU KNOW...** which player is the tallest?

# Truth
# or Dare

**TRUTH** Have you ever toilet papered someone's house? Whose? Why?

**DARE** Don't use your hands for the next three minutes.

**DO YOU KNOW...** which player has visited the most states in the United States?

---

**TRUTH** What would you most like to change about yourself?

**DARE** You're John Travolta and you've got *Saturday Night Fever.* Dance.

**DO YOU KNOW...** which player has keys in his/her pocket?

# Truth or Dare

**39**

**TRUTH** Name the animal the player to your right most resembles and tell why.

**DARE** Do a backward somersault.

**DO YOU KNOW...** which player prefers mayo to mustard?

— · — · — · — · — · —

**40**

**TRUTH** What makes you sad?

**DARE** It's between you and four other Miss America finalists. Tell the judges your one wish for the world.

**DO YOU KNOW...** which players like iced tea?

# Truth or Dare

**TRUTH** What do you fight about most with your family?

**DARE** Pretend you are an aerobics instructor. Give a one-minute class.

**DO YOU KNOW...** which player has had a secret admirer?

_._._._._._._

**TRUTH** Are you happy with where you are in life? Why/why not?

**DARE** Balance on your hands and rest your knees on your elbows for three seconds.

**DO YOU KNOW...** which players take daily vitamins?

# Truth
# or Dare

**TRUTH** What do you think would be the worst way to die?

**DARE** Push your cheeks together and tell a story about a boy named Chubby.

**DO YOU KNOW...** which players prefer pie and which prefer cake?

—·—·—·—·—·—

**TRUTH** What is the smell you most dislike? Be specific.

**DARE** Let the player to your left lick his/her finger and stick it in your ear (otherwise known as a "wet willie").

**DO YOU KNOW...** which player has had head lice?

# Truth or Dare

**45**

**TRUTH** How many times a day do you look at yourself in the mirror?

**DARE** Call your ex and pretend like you never broke up.

**DO YOU KNOW...** which player loves spicy foods?

- - - - - - -

**46**

**TRUTH** What is one talent most people here don't know that you have?

**DARE** Bases are loaded, it's the bottom of the ninth. As the third base coach, direct the batter how to hit. (No words, please.)

**DO YOU KNOW...** who's a cat person and who's a dog person?

# Truth
or Dare

**47**

**TRUTH** Name three things that turn you off.

**DARE** You're a magic lantern. Let the player to your right rub your tummy and make three wishes.

**DO YOU KNOW...** the job title of one of the other players?

— · — · — · — · — · —

**48**

**TRUTH** Ever get caught cheating? Give details.

**DARE** Phone a friend and ask for advice about whether or not you should invest in a new pair of socks.

**DO YOU KNOW...** which player can tell you what state you'd be in if you were at Niagara Falls? (Answer: New York)

# Truth or Dare

**TRUTH** If you could have any view from your bedroom window, what would it be?

**DARE** Put a towel or coat around your shoulders and say "because I am Superman" after everything you say for the next five minutes.

**DO YOU KNOW...** in what sport the player to your right could kick your butt?

—·—·—·—·—·—

**TRUTH** If you could knock someone down a few pegs, who would it be?

**DARE** Find a mirror and sweet talk yourself into going out on a date. Seal the deal with a big kiss.

**DO YOU KNOW...** which player dislikes broccoli?

# Truth or Dare

**TRUTH** What's the most embarrassing thing that's ever happened to you?

**DARE** It is your last lift in the Olympic weightlifting finals. Let's see you lift it—expression and grunting counts!

**DO YOU KNOW...** which player considers him/herself creative?

—·—·—·—·—·—

**TRUTH** What's your pin number?

**DARE** Call a friend and ask to speak to Jim Shorts.

**DO YOU KNOW...** which player cleaned his/her toilet most recently?

# Truth or Dare

**TRUTH** Tell whether each player is an optimist or a pessimist.

**DARE** Let the player to your right "accidentally" spill a small glass of water in your lap.

**DO YOU KNOW...** which player has been nabbed for speeding?

———————

**TRUTH** Which player would you hate to have as a parent?

**DARE** Act out the life of a mosquito in pantomime—birth through death.

**DO YOU KNOW...** which player reads comic books?

# Truth or Dare

**55**

**TRUTH** Tell the player to your left what your first impression of him/her was.

**DARE** Ask the other players to pick a "guitar rock" song for you. Then stand up and play a mean air guitar while you sing a few bars of that song.

**DO YOU KNOW...** what movie the player to your right last saw?

—·—·—·—·—·—

**56**

**TRUTH** If you could choose any time period to live in, which would it be?

**DARE** Wow, you're a model! Walk the catwalk singing "I'm a Model" and show off your haute couture.

**DO YOU KNOW...** how many siblings each player has?

# Truth or Dare

**57**

**TRUTH** What would you change in the world if you could only change one thing?

**DARE** You're a rapper. Make up a rap about how much you love clean socks.

**DO YOU KNOW...** which player has had poison ivy?

—·—·—·—·—·—

**58**

**TRUTH** Other than water, what liquid would you choose to drown in if you had to pick one?

**DARE** There's a new dance craze called the "Pork Rind" sweeping the nation. Show us how it goes.

**DO YOU KNOW...** which players paint their toenails?

# Truth or Dare

**TRUTH** If you could only have one of the five senses (sight, hearing, touch, smell, taste), which one would it be?

**DARE** Prove your existence by convincing everyone that, "I ____, therefore I am." Player to your right fills in the blank.

**DO YOU KNOW...** what costume the player to your right wore last Halloween?

—·—·—·—·—·—

**TRUTH** Which player is most likely to lie about his/her age?

**DARE** Do a convincing ad for poison ivy medication.

**DO YOU KNOW...** which player is most likely to donate to charity?

# Truth or Dare

**TRUTH** If you could win any existing award, what would it be? Why?

**DARE** Do your best imitation of a sad clown after a few too many drinks.

**DO YOU KNOW...** which player enjoys camping?

— · — · — · — · — · —

**TRUTH** If you had one million dollars to spend in only ONE store, what store would you choose?

**DARE** You're Tarzan and the player to your right is Jane. Tell Jane why she should marry you.

**DO YOU KNOW...** which players sleep with their pet?

# Truth or Dare

**TRUTH**  Ever eavesdrop on someone's phone call? If so, whose call?

**DARE**  Stand in the "pose of a tree" yoga position for the next two minutes. Don't know it? Make it up.

**DO YOU KNOW...** which players have been inside a police car?

—·—·—·—·—·—

**TRUTH**  If you could be a fly on a wall for a day, whose wall would you like to hang out on?

**DARE**  Do a 360° spin while standing on your head.

**DO YOU KNOW...** which player would try skydiving?

# Truth or Dare

**TRUTH** If you woke up and saw your name on the front page, what would you want the caption to say?

**DARE** Imitate Augustus Gloop from *Willie Wonka and the Chocolate Factory* singing "I've Got a Golden Ticket."

**DO YOU KNOW...** which player likes spinach?

— · — · — · — · — · —

**TRUTH** Which player's mind would you most like to read right now?

**DARE** There's a new dance craze called the "Pork-N-Beans" sweeping the nation. Show us how it goes.

**DO YOU KNOW...** what ice cream flavor is the player to your left's favorite?

# Truth
# or Dare

**TRUTH** If you could trade families with someone in the room, who would it be?

**DARE** Say "red leather, yellow leather" as fast as you can 10 times.

**DO YOU KNOW...** what the name of the player to your left's first grade teacher was?

--- --- --- ---

**TRUTH** Your boy/girlfriend dumps you after being cast in a Hollywood blockbuster. Do you sell those compromising photos to the tabloids?

**DARE** Play "This Little Piggy" on one of the other players. Socks off!

**DO YOU KNOW...** which player is least likely to sneak into the movies?

# Truth or Dare

**TRUTH** If the player to your left were a dog, what breed would s/he be? Why?

**DARE** You're the teacher. Give the other players a lesson on how to blow their noses.

**DO YOU KNOW…** which player has tried dog food?

—·—·—·—·—·—

**TRUTH** Which player most reminds you of one of your grammar school teachers? Why?

**DARE** Ask "Would you like fries with that?" after everything you say for the next five minutes.

**DO YOU KNOW…** which player has been to the symphony?

# Truth or Dare

**71**

**TRUTH** How old would you like to be when you die?

**DARE** It's your final audition for the musical *Annie*. Do your best song and dance performance of "Tomorrow."

**DO YOU KNOW...** which player gets into an elevator without letting the people out first?

—·—·—·—·—·—

**72**

**TRUTH** Name the one person you would nominate for sainthood, if you could.

**DARE** Let the player to your left pluck a hair from your arm.

**DO YOU KNOW...** which players have piercings?

# Truth or Dare

**TRUTH**  Which player would be the hardest to live with? Why?

**DARE**  Do the traditional Russian dance, the "Cossack" (arms folded while squatting and kicking at the same time).

**DO YOU KNOW...** which player can point north?

—·—·—·—·—·—

**TRUTH**  What's the last good deed you've done?

**DARE**  Do a back bend.

**DO YOU KNOW...** which player has ever met anyone famous?

# Truth or Dare

**TRUTH** Name the person that you think was most influential in rock and roll music.

**DARE** Walk in a crabwalk across the room while balancing a piece of fruit on your stomach.

**DO YOU KNOW...** which player can ride a skateboard?

— · — · — · — · — · —

**TRUTH** Describe the last time you were truly frightened.

**DARE** After a big Chinese meal everyone looks forward to his/her fortune cookie. Tell each player his/her fortune.

**DO YOU KNOW...** which player can talk a starving dog off a meat wagon?

# Truth or Dare

**TRUTH** Describe in detail what you wore to your first school dance.

**DARE** Lie on your stomach and grab your feet with your hands.

**DO YOU KNOW...** which player can program his/her VCR?

—·—·—·—·—·—

**TRUTH** What would be the first three words you would teach a parrot, if you had one?

**DARE** In an Irish accent say, "I've found the pot of gold at the end of the rainbow!" and click your heels together like a lucky leprechaun.

**DO YOU KNOW...** which player is most likely to make a new friend?

# Truth or Dare

**TRUTH** If you were a cat, who would you like your owner to be?

**DARE** Lie on your side and do 20 leg lifts while singing whatever the player to your left tells you to.

**DO YOU KNOW. . .** which player is most likely to be a contestant on a game show?

— · — · — · — · — · —

**TRUTH** If you could be good friends with a celebrity, who would it be?

**DARE** There's a new dance craze called the "Mullet Man" sweeping the nation. Show us how it goes.

**DO YOU KNOW. . .** which player has the largest CD collection?

# Truth or Dare

**81**

**TRUTH** What's the best song you could wake up to?

**DARE** You've just come across the player to your left's diary. Read a juicy passage out loud to the group.

**DO YOU KNOW...** which player has the best poker face?

— · — · — · — · — · —

**82**

**TRUTH** If you wrote your memoir, what would the title be?

**DARE** You're a stag. Leap across the room.

**DO YOU KNOW...** which player can spell "supercalifragilisticexpiali-docious" out loud?

# Truth
# or Dare

**TRUTH** What's the most reckless thing you've ever done?

**DARE** Pretend the player to your left is a big baby and burp him/her.

**DO YOU KNOW...** which player was a bedwetter?

—·—·—·—·—·—

**TRUTH** Which emotion would you eliminate from existence if you could pick one?

**DARE** You're the spokesperson for a new product called "Meat Sticks." Sell it to the other players.

**DO YOU KNOW...** which player always hangs up his/her clothes?

# Truth or Dare

**TRUTH** Which player is different than you thought they were, based on your first impression?

**DARE** You're at a heavy metal concert. Shout over the music till your next turn.

**DO YOU KNOW...** what the player to your left has on his/her key chain other than keys?

---

**TRUTH** What's the one burden you wish you could free yourself from?

**DARE** Do an interpretive dance that expresses your feelings about the player to your left.

**DO YOU KNOW...** which player won't blow his/her nose in public?

# Truth or Dare

**TRUTH** Describe a time you felt like a real dork.

**DARE** Remember your favorite song when you were 12? Good—now sing it.

**DO YOU KNOW...** which player blow dries his/her hair?

—————————

**TRUTH** If the player to your left had a personalized license plate, what would it be?

**DARE** Make up a song about the person sitting next to you, then sing it.

**DO YOU KNOW...** which player eats sushi?

# Truth or Dare

**TRUTH** If the United States had to sacrifice one state, which state would you give away?

**DARE** Play dingdong ditch (ring the doorbell and run) on a next-door neighbor.

**DO YOU KNOW...** which player has hairy armpits?

—·—·—·—·—·—

**TRUTH** What grade in school was toughest for you?

**DARE** Make up the chorus to a heavy metal ballad, then croon it to someone in the room.

**DO YOU KNOW...** which player has been to Mexico?

# Truth
# or Dare

**TRUTH** Which member of your family is most likely from outer space?

**DARE** Imitate your kindergarten teacher giving instructions about using the toilet properly.

**DO YOU KNOW...** which player has cheated when playing hide-and-seek?

— · — · — · — · — · —

**TRUTH** Which player's dad would you say was a ladies' man when he was younger?

**DARE** Identify one thing the player to your right has that you want, then beg that person for it.

**DO YOU KNOW...** which player has pit stains on his/her t-shirts?

# Truth or Dare

**TRUTH** What was your mom's pet name for you when you were little?

**DARE** Act out a scene where the person to your right gets arrested. You play cop.

**DO YOU KNOW...** which player followed *90210* from the Brenda years to its finale?

— · —· —· —· —· —

**TRUTH** Have you ever not left a tip in a restaurant?

**DARE** Make up a rap song about your least favorite teacher (or boss) ever.

**DO YOU KNOW...** which player picks out his/her outfit for the day the night before?

# Truth
# or Dare

**TRUTH** Have you ever picked wax out of your ear in a public place?

**DARE** Imitate the person on your left getting caught in a lie.

**DO YOU KNOW...** which player owns a boy band CD?

———————

**TRUTH** Have you ever told someone you aced a test when you really bombed it?

**DARE** You just got a television commercial time slot for your *Best Breakup Songs* double disk compilation. Convince the other players to order by sampling some songs.

**DO YOU KNOW...** who would rather cheat than lose?

# Truth or Dare

**97**

**TRUTH** Describe what you wore in your third-grade class picture.

**DARE** Stuff a pillow down the back of your pants. Now ask the player to your left, "Does this make me look fat?"

**DO YOU KNOW...** which player showers with his/her watch on?

—·—·—·—·—·—

**98**

**TRUTH** Describe your worst nervous habit.

**DARE** Belch. Loudly.

**DO YOU KNOW...** which player can't hold a grudge?

# Truth or Dare

**99**

**TRUTH** Have you ever laughed so hard that your drink came out your nose?

**DARE** You're a sportscaster. Announce where you are and what each player is wearing.

**DO YOU KNOW...** which player is camera shy?

— · — · — · — · —

**100**

**TRUTH** If you could take singing lessons from any famous singer, who would you pick as your teacher?

**DARE** Try to do the "lotus" yoga pose. If you don't know it, make it up.

**DO YOU KNOW...** which player cries at commercials?

# Truth or Dare

**101**

**TRUTH** Which player is most likely to make you laugh so hard you pee in your pants?

**DARE** Do your best imitation of E.T., the Extraterrestrial.

**DO YOU KNOW...** which player has tried romance with a friend and failed?

-- -- -- -- -- -- -- --

**102**

**TRUTH** Which player would be most likely to be named class clown in a high school yearbook?

**DARE** Do a happy dance.

**DO YOU KNOW...** which player would say s/he has a quick temper?

# Truth or Dare

**TRUTH** Confess the one lie you've told that you feel most guilty about.

**DARE** Pretend that you're so dizzy you can barely stand up straight.

**DO YOU KNOW...** which player would eat a candy bar for breakfast?

—·—·—·—·—

**TRUTH** Describe one time that you tortured an insect.

**DARE** You're a fifteenth-century explorer. Claim this land in the name of your country!

**DO YOU KNOW...** which player likes maraschino cherries?

# Truth or Dare

**TRUTH** Who in the room do you think would be voted "Most Bossy"?

**DARE** Pretend that you're a photographer. Take a memorable photo of the group.

**DO YOU KNOW...** which player would rather hit the beach than the slopes?

—·—·—·—·—·—·—

**TRUTH** Have you ever snuck into a movie?

**DARE** Pretend to parallel park and bump fenders with the players on either side of you.

**DO YOU KNOW...** which player has a cookie recipe memorized?

# Truth or Dare

**TRUTH** Which would be harder to give up: ice cream or potato chips?

**DARE** Using your body as an instrument, play "Jingle Bells."

**DO YOU KNOW...** which player can name four *Peanuts* characters?

— · — · — · — · — · — · —

**TRUTH** Which player would make the best cop?

**DARE** Yell "Watch out, pregnant lady comin' thru!" out the window at the top of your lungs.

**DO YOU KNOW...** which player is never a member of the clean plate club?

# Truth
# or Dare

**TRUTH**  While driving along the highway, you notice a car pulled over to the side with a flat tire. What do you do?

**DARE**  Walk across the room like you've got a stick up your bottom.

**DO YOU KNOW...** which player knows that a royal flush has nothing to do with a toilet? And can prove it?

— · — · — · — · — · —

**TRUTH**  Your son's beachball blows into the lake while you're packing the car to go home. If you jump in now, you can still catch it. What do you do?

**DARE**  You've gotta go and someone's in the bathroom. Let us see you hold it till your next turn.

**DO YOU KNOW...** which players are wearing a belt? No peeking!

# Truth or Dare

**TRUTH** Have you ever pretended to be someone else? Why?

**DARE** Develop an allergy to your own shirt.

**DO YOU KNOW...** which player is a secret slob—and will admit it?

———————————

**TRUTH** You borrowed a ring from a friend and lost it. Do you replace the ring without letting her know or do you tell her?

**DARE** You are joined at the hip, literally, to the player on your right for the next three minutes.

**DO YOU KNOW...** which player is most likely to cry while peeling an onion?

# Truth or Dare

**TRUTH** Which player is most generous?

**DARE** You're a farmer. Call your pigs to their morning slop.

**DO YOU KNOW...** which players have dirt under their fingernails?

—·—·—·—·—·—

**TRUTH** What would you do if you saw your best friend's significant other kissing someone else?

**DARE** You're a chicken about to be beheaded for tonight's dinner. Escape your fate!

**DO YOU KNOW...** which player likes Mountain Dew®?

# Truth
# or Dare

**115**

**TRUTH** Have you ever had a dream about someone else in the room?

**DARE** Pantomime the act of applying lotion all over your body.

**DO YOU KNOW...** which player didn't have a Valentine this year?

---

**116**

**TRUTH** Have you ever lied to your friends or family about who you voted for in an election?

**DARE** In quick succession, imitate three different barnyard animals. Now do it again!

**DO YOU KNOW...** which player's parents are still together?

# Truth or Dare

**TRUTH** A person you don't like offers to help you move. Do you let him/her help you?

**DARE** Pretend to eat cookies like you're Cookie Monster.

**DO YOU KNOW...** which player can count to 10 in French?

—·—·—·—·—·—

**TRUTH** You're getting HBO without paying for it. Do you keep it or say something?

**DARE** Senator, you've just been accused of taking bribes. What do you have to say to the press?

**DO YOU KNOW...** which player knows the theme song from *Grease*?

# Truth or Dare

**TRUTH** If you could have lunch with one person from any time in history, who would it be?

**DARE** Take out all of the money in your wallet/purse and count it in front of all of the other players.

**DO YOU KNOW...** which player reads *People* magazine?

—·—·—·—·—·—

**TRUTH** Would you rather be the Joker or Batman?

**DARE** Pretend you are a cheerleader and do a cheer for the others.

**DO YOU KNOW...** which player thinks *Dude, Where's My Car?* is a good movie?

# Truth or Dare

**TRUTH** You see a lost dog wandering in and out of traffic. Do you stop and help?

**DARE** Turn your shirt around without taking it off.

**DO YOU KNOW...** which player stays up late enough to watch Letterman?

------·--·--·--·--·------

**TRUTH** If you're in a big hurry and you see that there's an easy way to cut in line, do you do it?

**DARE** Make three sounds that are usually related to being in the bathroom.

**DO YOU KNOW...** which player drives a stick shift?

# Truth
# or Dare

**TRUTH** You go to your college reunion and someone you don't recognize is very happy to see you. What do you do?

**DARE** Name two U.S. states that begin with the word "South."

**DO YOU KNOW...** which player's dad has a moustache?

— · — · — · — · — · —

**TRUTH** Would you borrow money from your child's piggy bank without telling him/her?

**DARE** Make up a convincing commercial for beef-flavored ice cream.

**DO YOU KNOW...** which player had a tree house/fort when s/he was a kid?

# Truth or Dare

**TRUTH**   Your friends Tom and Jane started dating five months ago. You know Jane just kissed Harry and isn't going to tell Tom. Do you spill the beans?

**DARE**   Pretend you're Harry Potter and tell us about your Nimbus 2000 broomstick in your best British accent.

**DO YOU KNOW...** which player grew up in the suburbs?

—·—·—·—·—·—

**TRUTH**   You and a friend have front row seats to see your favorite band. Halfway through the show, your friend gets a migraine and needs to go home. What do you do?

**DARE**   Use whistling as your only form of communication until your next turn.

**DO YOU KNOW...** which player can quote a line from *Casablanca*?

# Truth or Dare

**TRUTH** You are auditioning for *Survivor*. What's the one thing about yourself that you'll tell the casting crew to make a lasting impression?

**DARE** Chew some candy or food and ask the others if they like "SEE FOOD" as you open your mouth for display.

**DO YOU KNOW...** which player should drink decaf, but doesn't?

**TRUTH** Describe the worst vacation you have ever had.

**DARE** Speak only in song until your next turn.

**DO YOU KNOW...** which player orders his/her toast dry?

# Truth or Dare

**TRUTH** If you could be a member of the opposite sex for one day, what would you do?

**DARE** Sing "I'm a Little Teapot" with all the actions.

**DO YOU KNOW...** which player is most likely to try something new?

— · — · — · — · —

**TRUTH** What would you set the national speed limit at, if you could change it?

**DARE** Impersonate the president.

**DO YOU KNOW...** which player is least likely to try something new?

# Truth or Dare

**TRUTH** What do you think is the most difficult thing about being a teenager today?

**DARE** Get down on your knees and sing "You Are My Sunshine" to the player on your left.

**DO YOU KNOW...** which player has been on a rollercoaster most recently?

—·—·—·—·—·—·—

**TRUTH** Name the most important quality in a friend.

**DARE** It's karaoke time! Sing a couple lines of your favorite song.

**DO YOU KNOW...** which player still watches cartoons?

# Truth
# or Dare

**TRUTH** If you had to work in one store at your local mall for the rest of your life, what store would you choose to work in?

**DARE** Spin in a circle 10 times.

**DO YOU KNOW...** which player likes to take catnaps?

—·—·—·—·—·—

**TRUTH** If you could skip one grade, which one would it be?

**DARE** Have a staring contest with the player to your right. Go the longest without blinking and win!

**DO YOU KNOW...** which player knows Puff Daddy's real name?
(Answer: Sean Combs)

# Truth or Dare

**TRUTH** If you could have anyone's voice, whose would you choose?

**DARE** There's a new dance craze called the "Boot Lick" sweeping the nation. Show us how it goes.

**DO YOU KNOW...** which player has a savings account?

—·—·—·—·—·—·—

**TRUTH** What's your favorite type of foreign accent?

**DARE** Make up the chorus to a country song and sing it with a southern twang.

**DO YOU KNOW...** which player can name at least four of the six *Friends*?

# Truth or Dare

**TRUTH** Name the one place you would take all of your friends to dinner, if you could take them anywhere.

**DARE** Lead everyone in the chant "We want to eat, eat a lot of meat!" at least six times.

**DO YOU KNOW...** which player can tell you what Marshall Mathers' stage name is? (Answer: Eminem)

—·—·—·—·—

**TRUTH** If you could change the number of siblings you have, what would you change it to?

**DARE** Pretend you are the Wicked Witch of the West and Dorothy has just poured water over your head. You're melting! You're melting!

**DO YOU KNOW...** which player knows what a tadpole turns into?

# Truth or Dare

**TRUTH** What physical characteristic about yourself reminds you of one of your parents?

**DARE** There's a new dance craze called the "Weiner Dog" sweeping the nation. Show us how it goes.

**DO YOU KNOW...** which player might someday be a famous author?

— — — — — — — —

**TRUTH** If you had to give everyone you know the same exact gift (excluding money) for the holidays next year, what would you give?

**DARE** Pretend to walk a tightrope.

**DO YOU KNOW...** which player has asked for an extension on a school paper more than once?

# Truth
# or Dare

**TRUTH** Which player has poor table manners?

**DARE** Play leapfrog over the other players while sticking out your tongue and saying "ribbit."

**DO YOU KNOW...** which player has rescued an injured animal?

---

**TRUTH** Describe the most difficult goodbye you ever had to say.

**DARE** Make up a convincing commercial for diet pound cake.

**DO YOU KNOW...** which player can name the first five presidents of the United States?

# Truth or Dare

**143**

**TRUTH** At what moment in your life were you most proud of yourself?

**DARE** How low can you go? Show the other players your lowest limbo.

**DO YOU KNOW...** which player likes to hang out with his/her parents?

---

**144**

**TRUTH** If you were offered the starring role in a major motion picture, but a requirement was to bare all for the camera, would you accept the part?

**DARE** You are a con artist. Make up your best story to convince the player to your left to give you $200.

**DO YOU KNOW...** which players have been windsurfing?

# Truth or Dare

**TRUTH** Describe a time you felt jealous when something good happened to one of your friends.

**DARE** Allow each player to pinch your cheeks and say, "Look how much you've grown!"

**DO YOU KNOW...** which player can dish it out, but can't take it?

— · — · — · — · — · —

**TRUTH** If life unfolded exactly as you'd like, where would you be in ten years?

**DARE** Sniff the player to your left's right armpit.

**DO YOU KNOW...** which player will say anything to get what s/he wants?

# Truth
# or Dare

**TRUTH** On a scale of 1 to 10, how do you rate?

**DARE** Let the player to your right use your lap as a foot rest for your next two turns.

**DO YOU KNOW...** which player could tell you what the English translation of Mardi Gras is? (Answer: Fat Tuesday)

—·—·—·—·—·—

**TRUTH** If a good friend needed $500 for a new leather coat and promised to pay you back as soon as she could, would you lend it to her?

**DARE** Sniff the player to your right's shoe.

**DO YOU KNOW...** which player had a Big Wheel® when s/he was a kid?

# LIAR'S CLUB

The game where honesty may or may not be the best policy...

**HOW TO BECOME A MEMBER OF THE LIAR'S CLUB:**
*Read a Liar's Club statement aloud to the group. Fill in the blank with either the truth or a convincing lie. Each player must guess whether you've told the truth or a lie. Collect a point for every player who guesses incorrectly. Whoever has the most points at the end of the game wins!*

1. I once dressed up as a _____ for Halloween.
2. I once received a_____ for my birthday.
3. The last book I read was_____.
4. I once called my best friend a _____ when I was mad at him/her.
5. I once _____-ed in public.
6. The weirdest thing that I ever ate was a(n) _____.
7. My favorite ice cream flavor is _____.
8. My biggest brush with fame was when I spotted _____ in _____.
9. I've been told that I look like _____.
10. I consider _____ to be a hidden talent of mine.
11. I once ate _____ pieces of pizza in one sitting.
12. I can list every album ever made by _____.
13. My dream job is _____.
14. If you looked under my bed, you'd find _____.

15. My _____ could really use a good cleaning.
16. The smell of _____ makes me want to gag.
17. My worst haircut was _____ .
18. One of my worst nightmares is _____ .
19. I got into serious trouble for _____ when I was younger.
20. The person I share my deepest secrets with is _____ .
21. When I was a kid I watched _____ regularly.
22. I know the theme song to _____ by heart.
23. I've been told I was a _____ child.
24. I won _____ when I was _____ .
25. The last song I listened to was _____ .
26. If I were stranded on a deserted island, I'd like _____ to be with me.
27. If my house were on fire, the first thing I'd grab would be _____ .
28. Mt last fortune cookie said _____ .
29. I think _____ is a real drag.
30. The household chore I dislike most is _____ .
31. I am allergic to _____ .
32. My radio is usually tuned to _____ .
33. If I could have lunch with one celebrity (living or dead), it would be _____ .
34. My favorite item of clothing is _____ .
35. I've been caught _____ .
36. My first crush was on _____ .
37. The most valuable thing I've ever lost was _____ .
38. I enjoy _____ , even though I know it's not good for me.
39. My favorite after-school snack is _____ .
40. I took _____ lessons when I was younger.

# ABOUT THE AUTHOR

Always ahead of the game, Bob Moog's newest undertaking is truly novel. As a game inventor, his credits include such favorites as Twenty Questions® and 30 Second Mysteries®. As the CEO of University Games, he has propelled the company he founded with his college pal into an international operation that now boasts five divisions and over 350 products. Whether hosting his radio show "Games People Play," advising MBA candidates, or inventing games, Bob sees work as serious fun. He now brings his flair for fun and learning to the bookshelf with the Spinner Book line.

# Enjoy Spinner Books?
# Get an original game!

## Find these games and more at

 **or your nearest toy store.**

**UNIVERSITY GAMES**

**2030 Harrison Street, San Francisco, CA 94110**
**1-800-347-4818, www.ugames.com**